Praise for *Getting Grit*

"Ever meet someone who is that magical combination of wise yet [...] strong yet sensitive, inspiring yet down to earth? That's Carolin[...] I know nobody who's thought more about how to apply the s[...] research on grit and achievement to our own lives!"

ANGELA DUCKWORTH
founder and Scientific Director, Character Lab; Christopher H. Browne
Distinguished Professor of Psychology, University of Pennsylvania

"*Getting Grit* is a remarkable collection of research and ideas for more achievement and well-being, starting today. An amazing work that captures the most practical ideas from positive psychology and beyond! The ultimate guide to living life with grit and without regret."

TOM RATH
author of *StrengthsFinder 2.0* and *Are You Fully Charged?*

"It's one thing to value grit—it's another to develop it. Caroline Miller has made that her life's work, and in this book she shares a series of useful steps for increasing your persistence for the right reasons in the right ways."

ADAM GRANT
author of *Originals* and *Give and Take*

"The minute I picked up *Getting Grit*, I feverishly began taking notes. Caroline Miller understands the essential truth that all women who want to be truly confident and who want to succeed need grit. It's a critical building block for both accomplishment and satisfaction. And Miller is the consummate grit coach—she motivates flawlessly with a blend of science and stories, humor, and challenge. Her recipe is the definitive guide to getting grit back into our lives."

CLAIRE SHIPMAN
coauthor of *The Confidence Code* and *Womenomics*

GETTING
grit

GETTING

grit

the **EVIDENCE-BASED APPROACH** to **CULTIVATING PASSION, PERSEVERANCE,** and **PURPOSE**

CAROLINE ADAMS MILLER

sounds true
BOULDER, COLORADO

Sounds True
Boulder, CO 80306

Some names and identifying details have been changed to protect the privacy
of individuals.

Published 2017

Cover design by Rachael Murray
Book design by Beth Skelley

Printed in Canada

Library of Congress Cataloging-in-Publication Data
Names: Miller, Caroline Adams, 1961- author.
Title: Getting grit : the evidence-based approach to cultivating passion,
    perseverance, and purpose / Caroline Miller.
Description: Boulder, Colorado : Sounds True, [2017] |
    Includes bibliographical references.
Identifiers: LCCN 2016046284 (print) | LCCN 2017004305 (ebook) |
    ISBN 9781622039203 (pbk.) | ISBN 9781622039210 (e-book)
Subjects: LCSH: Determination (Personality trait) | Perseverance (Ethics) |
    Self-realization.
Classification: LCC BF698.35.D48 M55 2017 (print) | LCC BF698.35.D48 (ebook) |
    DDC 171/.3—dc23
LC record available at https://lccn.loc.gov/2016046284

10 9 8 7 6 5 4 3 2 1

To all of the wise, wonderful, recovering people in my first twelve-step community, whose role modeling, friendship, and mentoring gave me the necessary ingredients to build authentic grit. My gratitude is boundless because I was given hope, which gave me back my life.

Contents

Introduction

In 2012, my oldest son, Haywood, graduated college with a degree in accounting. To select the right university for his strengths and interests, he followed his major consuming passion, swimming. He started at the University of Maryland on a partial scholarship and transferred halfway through, to the University of Cincinnati, so that his best swimming events matched the holes in their roster. His final GPA was okay—not phenomenal—so I was a bit surprised when he was asked to interview at almost every major accounting firm in the country.

In the midst of a difficult job market and the lingering effects of the recession, we were prepared for Haywood to have to move home, like so many of his peers. The word on the street was that he'd be stymied in getting a job that would allow him to live independently and begin to attack his student loans—or to get any job at all. I was happily taken aback when my son immediately landed a job at one of the best accounting firms in the country with a starting salary that made his living alone more than doable.

Curious, I asked him what he thought had made him a winning candidate when the media had painted a picture of a job market so bleak that we all assumed only the cream of the crop from the very top schools would find employment. Haywood mused for a moment, and then answered: "I think it was the swimming. The only questions I was really asked to elaborate on were about how many years I'd spent practicing, whether it was once or twice a day, the fact that I'd competed through college, and that I was elected captain of my college team despite transferring in my junior year." He continued, "I think they just wanted to know if I had a work ethic, leadership qualities, and the ability to get along with people," and then added with a laugh, "My GPA obviously wasn't the deciding factor!"

I shouldn't have been too surprised by his good news in light of the work I do with high-performance individuals around the world on goal-setting and emotional flourishing, but as an anxious mom, I still worried that Haywood's decision to focus on swimming in college may not have been the best idea for his employment future. In this case, though, his desirability mirrored what has increasingly occurred in today's job market, and what I wrote about in my book *Creating Your Best Life*. In it, I noted that many in the generation of Millennials, raised on mountains of trophies and self-esteem-building ceremonies, were turning out to be a disaster in the working world, and that employers were hiring consultants to coach them on how to work diligently and take feedback when their performance was anything other than "awesome."

To avoid these types of problems, firms were increasingly coming up with unique ways to discern which candidates would bring a strong work ethic, good sense of teamwork, and likeability to their company, and not problems that would necessitate firing these employees later. Instead of focusing on GPAs and summer internships, they wanted people like my son, who had nursed a passion for years, and stuck with the activity even when it was difficult and, often, the only reward was the satisfaction of not giving up. The thinking is that if these types of job applicants have already learned how to work hard, overcome disappointment, and persist in the absence of constant praise, then they'll be the kinds of employees who can be trained to do almost anything.

My interest in the topic of grit was ignited during the year I spent at the University of Pennsylvania, from 2005 to 2006, earning one of the first master's of applied positive psychology (MAPP) degrees in the burgeoning field of applied positive psychology—the science of happiness. There, I was introduced to the work of Angela Duckworth, who was pursuing her doctorate under Dr. Martin Seligman on a quality she was calling "grit," which she defined as "passion and perseverance in pursuit of long-term goals." As someone who had spent several decades writing about and coaching others on how to set and achieve difficult goals, I was mesmerized by the scientific findings I learned at Penn concerning what it takes to be a "winner" in some of life's most challenging arenas. I became steeped in concepts like goal-setting theory, self-efficacy theory, and social contagion, and I began to link all of these ideas together in a new way, which morphed from my capstone project into my book *Creating Your Best Life*. In that book, I included a chapter on Angela's research and findings, which weren't generally known outside of academia at that time.

I wrote that Angela's twelve-item Grit Scale had been found to be the leading predictor of who drops out at West Point during the first summer, known as "Beast Barracks." It had also worked with preteens, determining who would reach the finals of the National Spelling Bee. Since *Creating Your Best Life* was published, the Grit Scale has been found to predict tenacity in other difficult situations, too: which men remain married, which inner-city students will complete high school, which cadets will be accepted into the United States Special Operations Forces, and even which economically disadvantaged students will graduate from college.

In the intervening years since I graduated from the MAPP program, I've worked with thousands of individuals as a professional coach, speaker, and educator. What I have heard and seen, including what I witnessed in my children's lives as they grew from infancy to adulthood in the middle of the now-maligned "self-esteem movement," has convinced me to add my voice and thoughts to the burgeoning field of grit commentary. I am also emboldened to speak up because I see youth and adults who are desperate to learn how to cultivate more grit in themselves, their workplaces, their families, and their communities. They want to help change the current standards of banal mediocrity back to rigorous excellence, but they say they don't know where to start or what to do to make that happen.

I think we can all agree that the world is facing challenges that are daunting and even unprecedented, and that a call for resilience of the highest order is facing us. Roiling international economic markets, random terrorist attacks, and global climate challenges are exacerbated by the twenty-four-hour news cycle that keeps negative news at the forefront at all times. U.S. college students are reporting epidemic levels of anxiety and depression, and on top of that, they are often mired in student-loan debt and negative prognoses about their future earning possibilities. Without grit, how can anyone survive or thrive?

What's in this book?

In this book, I share research and ideas about how we can boost the character strengths and behaviors that we see in gritty people. I've even come up with a term that I use to describe the type of grit I think elicits the greatest results: "authentic grit." I define this as "the passionate pursuit of hard goals that awes and inspires others to become better people, flourish emotionally, take positive risks, and live their best lives."

The book is divided into two parts. The first is about different types of grit—both good and bad—and how our nation came to embrace and amplify mediocrity in many arenas and what that has left us to work with. The second section covers my observations, experience, and some of the research on how we can build the strengths and actions that comprise authentic grit, such as passion, goal-setting, self-regulation, confidence, risk-taking, and patience, among others. You'll also find exercises throughout these chapters—some for you to use on your own and many you can use in a variety of settings with others—to set goals, develop a resilient mind-set, create winning strategies, assemble supportive teams and communities, and raise standards that awe and inspire others to their own greatness. These are user-friendly ideas and resources that you can use again and again.

My overarching goal in this book is to demonstrate that building authentic grit isn't just possible but that it's our duty to do so if we want to live in a world that upholds standards of excellence and shuns quitting. We need resilience, optimism, and determination to overcome setbacks that threaten our flourishing and peace, and we need to arm the next generation—the first in U.S. history predicted not to have the same standard of living as their parents—with the science of happiness and the tools to persevere toward their best and most meaningful lives.

With the information I share here, and the ongoing research findings from places like Angela Duckworth's Character Lab, the Greater Good Science Center, the Center for Healthy Minds, and the University of Pennsylvania's Positive Psychology Center, I believe we can begin to imagine and create a world that makes us proud and that uplifts us to be bolder, more tenacious, and more inspirational. When we learn how to set the right goals and see them through to the finish line, become comfortable with discomfort, and use setbacks as springboards, we can live with passion, purpose, and perseverance. When that happens, having the right kind of grit won't be a fantasy. It will be the reality that more of us live and share with others so that we can all become better versions of ourselves.

Let's get started!

part 1

Can You Spell G-R-I-T?

every spring in Washington, DC, there are two occurrences we look forward to: the cherry blossoms that explode in frothy white beauty around the National Mall, and the Scripps National Spelling Bee. Founded in 1925, the Bee is a popular nationwide contest open to students as young as six and as old as fourteen, hundreds of whom descend on the city after winning regional bees in their state. Contestants are winnowed down through preliminary rounds, and the final rounds are televised live.

A sports channel, ESPN covers the nerve-wracking competition with as much diligence and thoroughness as they bring to other athletic contests. It's easy to understand why they do so after watching the Bee for just a few minutes. The same kinds of stresses and mental demands that mature athletes face in competition are on display here, but among boys and girls, most of whom haven't hit puberty yet. One at a time, kids in braces, kids with acne, and girls with jaunty bows on top of their heads come silently to the front of the stage, some needing to stand on a chair to reach the microphone, and they're asked to spell some of the most arcane words on the planet. They have to do all of this under hot lights and the pressure of time, one letter at a time, while millions of viewers watch them and the children's parents gulp, perspire, and pray from the audience. Because of the contestants' excellent preparation, this can go on for hours and hours, round after round, sometimes late into the night, as it has for the last several years. Starting in 2014, the Bee has had to name co-champions because they couldn't stump some relentless finalists, who hung on through fourteen rounds until the Bee ran out of words to quiz them on.

Time magazine did a story on some of the Bee's former winners in a "Where Are They Now?" feature, in May 2016, and found that many had gone on to be successful professionals, often blazing pathways in the fields of education, investment, journalism, medicine, and economics. They credited their years of spelling competition with lifelong benefits, especially their preparation for and participation in the nerve-wracking National Spelling Bee. Wendy Guey Lai said that studying for the Bee taught her how to be "resilient, detail-oriented, and exhibit grace under pressure." Pratyush Buddiga said that he'd become good at "pattern recognition" and "trusting my gut instincts." Balu Natarajan, who won the Bee on his third try, noted that the competition is more like "a marathon and not a sprint," and said that his professional career in sports medicine had been impacted by the Bee: "It takes years for most of the kids to hold up that trophy or make it to the national competition. That's what allowed me to have an appreciation for endurance athletes and enjoy taking care of them."[1]

When Angela Duckworth was beginning to refine her study of the personality trait she called "grit" at the University of Pennsylvania in 2005, she wondered if the resilient and determined kids she and everyone else saw on television possessed the quality she was defining as "passion and perseverance in pursuit of long-term goals." So she was permitted access to the 273 participants in the 2005 Bee, over half of whom agreed to fill out forms and submit to questions about their work habits, intelligence, and number of years competing in spelling contests. She also administered her newly developed Grit Scale, which contained statements such as "I often choose a goal but later decide to pursue a different one," and "I have overcome setbacks to accomplish an important challenge." After the results were crunched, self-control was an important success factor, but when the age of the participants was factored out, the Grit Scale was the leading predictor of who reached the finals of the Bee. Later parsing of the data showed that much of what nurtured the grit was failing to advance one year, which meant that those students went home and studied even harder, doing much of it on weekends in solitary study.

One year later, Duckworth and her colleagues administered the Grit Scale, as well as a battery of other tests, to 976 incoming West Point freshmen. After teasing out factors like self-control, IQ, and other measures of excellence, the Grit Scale more accurately predicted the cadets who dropped out of Beast Barracks—the hellish first summer of training—than previously used measures, such as the Whole Candidate Score, composed of things like academic honors, leadership recommendations, and grade-point averages. Although the difference was small, it was noteworthy, and when added to the National Spelling Bee findings, people suddenly wanted to know more about what was going on in Angela's lab at Penn.

The quality du jour

No matter where you turn now, grit has become the quality du jour. Grit is the "X" factor that people long to understand and nurture in themselves and others. Honored with a 2013 MacArthur "Genius" Grant, Duckworth and her presentations about grit are staples at education, leadership, and psychology conferences, and one of her speeches, "The Power of Passion and Perseverance," is one of the most popular TED talks ever posted online. Her book, *Grit*, published in 2016, rocketed to the top of the bestseller lists the week it came out, and President Obama mentioned it in two State of the Union addresses; he also made the cultivation of grit in the classroom his Department of Education's top priority in 2013.

As promising as her work is, Duckworth has concerns about how some have rushed ahead to use grit in ways that she doesn't think are ready to be implemented. For example, some schools are eagerly rolling out tests for grit, saying that students and teachers will be evaluated on their grit, even though it's not clear how to do that in schools or if it's even the right measure for every student in every setting. Low-income students who have to overcome daily obstacles just to go to school may not benefit from having their grit evaluated, and instead may get more value from building up their self-efficacy and hope. Paul Tough, who has studied grit and written *How Children Succeed: Grit, Curiosity, and the Hidden Power of Character,* finds that it might be more rewarding for these students to have family interventions that help parents learn how to manage frustration and anger, which could spawn cultures of love, acceptance, and warmth at home.[2]

Still, there's no question that Duckworth is on to something. Her study of legions of successful men and women across multiple domains, including investment banking, swimming, football, and chess, has found that there are common denominators in all of these people that are worth unpacking so that we can learn how to emulate their approach to their goals. She found that the people who had distinguished themselves in overcoming multiple challenges over many years to sustain the pursuit of something that was important to them had several critical qualities in common, namely:

- **Passion.** They were lit up from within by a cause or an activity that electrified and energized them, sometimes from a young age. They weren't guided by what others wanted; instead, they were single-mindedly focused on something that crowded out other interests, gave their lives meaning, and filled them with a sense of purpose.

- **Perseverance.** They weren't just resilient in the short run. They had a bounce-back quality that existed throughout years of emotional droughts, physical and financial setbacks, and discouragements that would cause many people to give up.

- **Long-term goals.** They attached a goal to their passion that might have seemed unrealistic to some, but that became their immovable North Star. In some cases, this led to world-renown or Olympic fame, but for others, the results were quieter, from regaining the ability to walk after a crippling injury, to maintaining the hope of being exonerated after wrongful incarceration, to remaining clean and sober in the hardest of circumstances.

Old wine in a new bottle?

Duckworth, who worked with her mentor, Marty Seligman—widely referred to as "the father of positive psychology"—to create the Grit Scale, believes that she has found a way to measure a unique, coveted quality that separates those who want to succeed at difficult goals from those who actually do it. The test teases out a variety of motivations and personality traits that are either related or unrelated to the qualities associated with being gritty. For example, someone can be tenacious and hardworking but not have a passion that translates into a deeply valued goal. By the same token, a person can be the epitome of passion but be unable to sustain focus on a hard goal through years of setbacks. Alternatively, someone might be hardworking and passionate but need external validation for achievement, and thus be unable to be resilient in the absence of trophies and renown.

Although similar to the quality called conscientiousness, which also predicts diligence, grit speaks to the type of behavior needed to be dutiful and disciplined in pursuit of a goal. Some of the criticism of the concept of grit has claimed that it is simply a restatement of conscientiousness—"old wine in a new bottle"—which Duckworth has ably defended as a very different construct with different outcomes. Among other points, she notes that conscientiousness isn't infused with the emotional fire that is so central to grit.

As a credentialed performance coach who works daily with people to help them understand and cultivate the type of energy and dedication needed to stick with and accomplish very difficult, life-changing goals, I agree wholeheartedly that conscientiousness simply doesn't cut it when you're talking about what it takes to set, pursue, and accomplish challenging and meaningful goals that profoundly change people's lives. Conscientiousness isn't the thing that keeps dreams alive when hope is fading, nor is it what is needed when you have to suddenly change course to adapt to new circumstances. In fact, I've seen conscientiousness overused to a person's detriment, which I call "stubborn grit."

How does the research help you and me?

I constantly sift through reams of research to figure out what I can do with it so that my clients have the right tools for change and success. Research is just research until someone like me comes along and extracts practical applications from it that people can readily understand and use in positive ways. To do what I do, and make a living at it, I have had to learn how to make an immediate difference in people's lives with whatever tools, motivation, and knowledge they need to get where they want to go. And when people state their most desired outcome for our work together, the development of more resilience and grit is often at the top of their list.

As a result, I have had to go far beyond the research on what people who are already gritty think and do in order to come up with a game plan for people who aren't there yet. I have to know what is *missing* in my clients' lives and why. I need to understand what happened in their family of origin that impacted their outlook, who currently supports their goals, what occurs around them now in their work and personal environments, and much more. If I don't know those variables, I can't diagnose the situation correctly and bring the right research and tools to our work.

So, while practitioners like me don't usually do academic research, we are accelerating the breakthroughs on grit as we work one on one with real people in many varied scenarios—from athletic fields to corporate offices—to see what works and what doesn't when it comes to changing for the better. And I believe that our results are as important to the study of grit as are the findings coming from academia, because without feedback from people like us, it's hard for the average person to take advantage of the statistic-laden research coming from universities and research labs all over the world.

For that reason, I pore through the research on grit, as well as the findings on such areas as passion, risk-taking, willpower, kindness, humility, savoring, goal-setting, and positive relationships, so that I can use the information effectively and efficiently with men and women, young and old, wherever they are in the change process. That's how I came up with my own definition of "authentic grit"—"the passionate pursuit of hard goals that awes and inspires others to become better people, flourish emotionally, take positive risks, and live their best lives." For me, grit isn't a positive unless it is a force for good. I think my definition captures the quality that I've seen produce excellent results and leave behind a worthwhile legacy. I'll say more about the elements that make up authentic grit in upcoming chapters to make it easier to understand how to cultivate it in new and unexpected ways.

Why does grit matter so much in the twenty-first century?

In recent years, a chorus of voices has gotten louder in the United States, lamenting the character and work ethic of many in the generation known as the Millennials, those born between the years 1980 and 2000. Dubbed the "Me Me Me Generation" by *Time* magazine, they have been roundly excoriated as the products of the misguided self-esteem movement, which encouraged parents to be friendly with their children and warmly praise them whenever possible.[3] Although this movement was well intended and meant to result in personal initiative and higher self-esteem, it has been a bust by every measure.

Exceptions are everywhere (I have raised three Millennials whom I admire very much), but psychologists say that by and large this generation is entitled and easily wounded by feedback or criticism, and that instead of having higher self-esteem and a sense of responsibility, they are fragile and narcissistic. Many value fame and money over meaning and purpose, seek shortcuts over hard work, and fold in the face of setbacks. Awash in creature comforts and quick fixes, they aren't likely to understand how to read maps or write properly without spell-check. And adults aren't viewed as guides but as equals, to whom they need not defer, partly because it's become acceptable to call teachers by their first name in many schools.

Anecdotal and evidence-based stories about the impact of this behavior are everywhere, and cause for grave concern in some quarters. Some psychologists note that the "dumbing down" of playgrounds into plastic contraptions surrounded by pillows of wood chips, so that children can avoid injuries and skinned knees, has created a generation of anxious adults who grew up afraid to climb trees or to take risks.[4] Some have even traced a drop in entrepreneurial activity in recent years to this phenomenon, noting that the age group that used to create new businesses and spark innovation has played it safer than previous generations, even after factoring in recessionary factors and a smaller middle class.[5]

The emphasis on nothing but high praise and perfect GPAs has also led to grade inflation in high school, university, and graduate-level settings, to the point that many companies say they can't rely on GPAs and degrees from elite schools to guarantee hardworking employees. Self-control has gone AWOL with dire consequences—a factor in American obesity rates that continue to skyrocket to all-time highs. The U.S. military has actually issued a report noting that American youth are "Too Fat to Fight." Sports coaches of professional teams lament that it's hard to get their well-paid athletes to pay attention at team meetings without taking away their smartphones, and some coaches have even quit their profession altogether, noting that the lack of a work ethic and willingness to sacrifice for the team have made many of the new players "uncoachable."[6]

Creating your best life requires grit

I have been working as a credentialed coach with high-performing individuals throughout the world for several decades, with a specialty in goal accomplishment. When I studied with Marty Seligman at the University of Pennsylvania in 2005, I was one of the first thirty-four people in the world to earn a master's in applied positive psychology (a MAPP degree, as you might recall from the introduction), also known as the science of happiness. As I noted earlier, that's when I was introduced to Angela Duckworth's fledgling research on grit, which I wove into my capstone project that year and which then became my book *Creating Your Best Life*. That book was the first to give readers ways to define and pursue meaningful paths to success and happiness that were grounded in research and academic theories—a feat Marty praised in his book *Flourish,* saying I'd added a "major missing piece" to the literature on success and goal accomplishment.[7]

I've come across a great deal of evidence that points toward the imperative of doing difficult things in order to live a satisfying, high-quality life filled with optimal achievement. For starters, I learned from Edwin Locke and Gary Latham, whose research has led to Goal Setting Theory, which holds that "challenging and specific" goals are required if someone wants to attain the highest levels of performance. (Easy goals, or "low goals," don't just result in mediocrity, they say, but also leave people feeling mediocre.[8]) From a theory of self-determination, proposed by Edward Deci and Richard Ryan, I discovered that people aren't happy doing nothing. We are driven to master our environments in order to feel related, autonomous, and competent, and when given the choice to do nothing over something, people overwhelmingly choose to be busy and productive.[9]

Newer research has found that at night we all scan our day for its highlights, especially noting what we are most proud of. As you might expect, the things that give us authentic self-esteem are never the activities or behaviors that are easy and inside our comfort zone. It's the difficult, challenging, and sometimes painful moments that leave us flush with a sense of pride and that make us more confident and hopeful about our capabilities and future.[10] And which two qualities have been found to most reliably predict success with our goals? Grit and curiosity.[11]

What will you regret?

When people come to me for help, they are often at a crossroads in life. Young or old, they are, in my observation, usually facing an important choice and want to proceed with support, accountability, and the guidance of a grounded professional. They aren't hesitating because they are contemplating doing something easy; it's always because there is something they want to do that is so far outside their comfort zone they have to be thoughtful and prepared about the plunge they're poised to take. And although they understand how hard the path will be, they also know that they won't ever be truly happy unless they give that goal a shot.

I can say without hesitation, after thousands of sessions with all kinds of men and women all over the world, that the people who are most satisfied with our coaching outcomes, and with themselves, are the ones who picked difficult goals and grew their grit to make a run for the brass ring. They leave our coaching as different people. I often tell friends that I feel like I work on the labor and delivery floor of a hospital because everyone is happy after they see the fruits of their labor. They are not just more confident after they cultivate grit and use it in a purposeful way—they are also more fulfilled.

Sometimes I get calls and pleas for help from people who, though they aren't 100 percent sure what they want to do, know that something is missing from their lives and that they can't continue on contentedly without exploring what else might be out there for them. At times like this, my go-to question is always, "When you are looking back on your life at the moment of death, what will you regret if you don't make any changes starting now?" The answers to that question have always borne fruit, and the goals that have emerged from those conversations have always been big ones that often involve inevitable upheavals, discomfort, and change. And in order to pursue and get to the finish line of those goals, it's been obvious that my clients need the elixir that Duckworth has now determined to be the unquestioned sign of elite excellence in punishing conditions: grit!

What if you don't have grit? Can you develop it?

The burning question in the psychology world right now is this very question: Can we cultivate grit? And if so, how? Early results and studies are pointing in some promising directions, not the least of which is the work by Stanford University social psychology researcher Carol Dweck, the author of *Mindset: The New Psychology of Success*. Dweck has found that when children grow up with praise for their innate intelligence—when things like solving a puzzle, drawing a picture, winning a race, or getting a good report card are met with responses like "You're so smart!" "You are awesome!" and "You deserve it!"—these children develop a "fixed mind-set," believing that their strengths and talents are fixed at birth. This leads them to avoid situations in which they might fail because they need to maintain the image and belief that they are special. Without that, it's hard for them to feel worthwhile.

On the other hand, children who grow up with praise for their effort, irrespective of outcome, develop a "growth mind-set." This means they learn to believe that even if they don't know something yet, with enough effort and persistence they can, over time, learn what doesn't come easily to them at first. These children develop more of a gritty approach to life and don't give up, even relishing the challenges put in front of them. They are also the ones who don't fold at the sign of discouragement or failure and who believe that outcomes are mostly under their control if they have enough persistence to keep going.

In her research on grit, Duckworth has also found that it is contagious, like many other behaviors, such as quitting smoking, gaining weight, and being happy. In fact, she says, West Point has found that cadets with lower grit scores have been found to benefit when they room with cadets who have higher grit scores, possibly because seeing someone work through frustration, find clever ways to delay gratification, or be resilient when faced with setbacks can rub off in positive ways. Most promising is that Duckworth and others note that grit has been found to increase over our lifespan, suggesting that it *is* a quality that benefits from specific interventions as well as the life experiences that result in wisdom.

Newer research: mirror neurons and virtual reality

Research on personality traits shows that some of our top strengths can be used to pursue goals in better and more strategic ways, maximizing our chances of getting past the tedium of learning something new as we develop "harmonious passion" for it, whether that's swimming or solving math problems. And research on self-regulation is finding myriad new ways we can cultivate willpower, from mindfulness practices to working with virtual avatars. In fact, I believe that the field of virtual reality is the most exciting field that has yet to be fully developed around grit cultivation, a topic I write more about later in the book.

There is also a wealth of data about how the brain works that wasn't available until recently, as well as batteries of tests that can "unpack" resilience. For example, research on mirror neurons is finding that it's easier to learn something new when we watch others do it. We also know from endurance tests that the body gives up only after the brain tells it to do so, opening the door to creative solutions that can help people "change the channel" in their brains when tempted to throw in the towel.[12] We also know that strategically located prompts, or cues—such as pictures or inspirational words—can make people either more disciplined or more lax in their efforts.[13] Agreeing to an "if-then" contract with yourself also triples your chances of accomplishing tough goals.[14]

What else contributes to building the grit muscle?

Since grit is contagious, can grow throughout a person's lifetime, and can be developed in the process of pursuing a big dream, it makes sense that its components can be isolated and then nurtured into flourishing abilities. Duckworth's definition of grit gives us clues about what we need to cultivate, including passion, resilience, and determined focus. But I believe we also need to take a look at the quality of our relationship skills, the prevalence of positive emotions in our lives, and our storehouse of willpower, among other elements, to develop the more well-rounded authentic grit. In my studies of gritty people, I've noticed that many of them have other critical qualities such as patience and curiosity, not to mention humility, an endearing quality that can attract the enthusiastic support of those who help them with their dreams over many years.

Why do I care so much?
My own story of getting grit

One of the reasons I feel so compelled to work in the field of motivation, goals, happiness, and grit is because I had the formula for finding success all wrong in the earlier part of my life, and suffered greatly as a result. Through failure and an early-adulthood reboot, however, I learned how to do what was necessary to find the right goals and summon up the perseverance to achieve them—and I developed grit in the process. My experience taught me that grit is definitely not a quality reserved for the select few; it is available to anyone who wants something so badly that they won't let anyone stop them until they've gone as far as they can, often achieving or coming close to that which they sought.

As a young girl in a privileged setting in the suburbs of Washington, DC, I was smart and talented according to IQ and other outward measures of success. That got me into the right schools with the right bumper stickers, but between the emphasis on appearing perfect in my family and the increasing pressures to perform in a variety of academic and extracurricular areas, I tried to protect myself from failure and the appearance of imperfection at all costs. As a result, I took shortcuts, most notably with food. Instead of being disciplined in my habits and training, I became bulimic, which was running rampant in my private school and my chosen sport of swimming.

As you may well know, bulimia is an eating disorder characterized by gorging on huge amounts of food followed by behaviors ranging from self-induced vomiting to laxative overdoses. For seven years, I lived a life of overeating, lying, hiding, and never really paying the full price for my binges, while maintaining a passable exterior. If I was persistent, it was only in making sure that my behavior remained secret and ongoing. Any attempts to stop or seek help were half-hearted, partly because there were no professionals who really knew how to "cure" it, and partly because it felt like a hopeless situation with no end anyway.

I graduated from Harvard University in 1983, and one week later I plunged right into marriage. It was only when I realized that attaining magna cum laude from an Ivy League school and marrying the handsome man of my dreams wasn't going to make me happy enough to overcome bulimia that I hit my last bottom. But in the depth of that misery in early 1984, I found the ingredients I needed to become a "paragon of grit," as Duckworth has kindly noted about my journey, which is chronicled in my TEDx talk "The Moments That Make Champions."

I decided I wanted to live more than I wanted to self-destruct, that I'd do whatever it took to get better, and that I wasn't going to stop until I found the right formula. Grit starts with passion, and I embraced a passion for living, for finding happiness outside of trying to have a perfect body, and for giving back to others instead of trying to figure out how I could come out the sole winner. "You can't keep what you don't give away" was the phrase I heard at my twelve-step group for compulsive eaters. If I had even one day of maintaining my abstinence from compulsive eating, I had something of value that could help someone else, which gave me purpose and humility.

For the first time, I learned how to persevere through temptation, emotional swings, setbacks, relapses, interpersonal challenges, and life's unending curveballs. I didn't resort to anything mood-altering during hard times, including food, alcohol, and recreational drugs; instead, I found ways to just sit with the uncomfortable feelings that I'd always buried. I shielded myself from people and places that weren't aligned with my goal of full health, and although I had no specific end date in mind, I just got up every day, week after week, month after month, year after year, and finally decade after decade, and did whatever I needed to do to get better.

In that process, I wrote two books about my path to complete recovery, *My Name Is Caroline* and *Positively Caroline,* which were the first autobiographies by anyone who had overcome bulimia and who had reached thirty years of recovery, respectively. Although I didn't have grit when I started on my journey, there's no question that I have it now. And because I know that life is sweeter and richer because I chose a difficult road and didn't quit until I reached a goal that mattered so much to me, I have a commitment to work with people on selecting and pursuing the goals that will light up their lives, and to help them cultivate grit, too. I believe that if I've been able to develop grit, others can, too, and that if I don't "give it away" and help others, I won't be able to "keep" what I've found and fully enjoy it.

Breast in Show

A few years ago on a languid August afternoon, a woman called me for help. She'd seen therapists and come to the realization that she didn't need to contemplate her childhood, her divorce, or whether she'd been a good mother. Instead, she needed to feel that her life was purposeful and meaningful—and her doctor suggested she call me because I would help her be accountable, to make the necessary changes for greater happiness and peace. The doctor knew that my approach would be different from anything this woman had encountered.

"What might you regret not doing when you're looking back on your life one day?" I asked her over the phone.

Her immediate answer: "I want to create the world's first musical about breast cancer."

I have been coaching for long enough to know that everyone has an unerring sense of what they lack or desire, and that my role is simply to challenge them in a variety of ways to unearth those facts and help them bring their aspirations to life. Besides, it would be ridiculous to implant dreams or hopes in others because it's impossible to be lit up by something that isn't intrinsically motivating. In fact, my clients' goals are so unique and personally galvanizing to them that I know I'd never be able to cook up anything more rewarding or satisfying than what I've been privileged to hear from them directly for so many years.

Two years later, that client, Eileen Mitchard, debuted *Breast in Show,* which garnered numerous awards, standing ovations, and raised thousands of dollars for cancer research. Although she was lit up with enthusiasm and energy from the success of the show, Eileen was set back with emergency heart surgery—but not for long. Within a year, she learned to row and started running, and when I last heard from her, she was routinely finishing 5K, 10K, and even half-marathon runs as she burst into her sixties, reborn with passion and focused on making each day count.

Eileen is a textbook example of what happens when people decisively choose a moment of change that separates their feeling ho-hum from their going for the gusto. Regardless of when that time comes—it could come after bottoming out with an eating disorder while young, failing at something in your middle age, or feeling purposeless in the empty nest—taking stock of your life and deciding to turn in a new direction can bear fruit that is life changing. And instead of running out of time to do this, we are now being gifted with another thirty years, on average, to make our retirement years richer than ever. Allianz Life Insurance has noted that the extra time many people now have is being used to "take a second chance at those life decisions you now regret."[15]

Over the years, I've had clients tell me they wanted to ride bareback in Mongolia along the Great Wall of China, become Olympic competitors, rise to be among the top one hundred people in their profession, ditch a lucrative career in computing to create a home-cooked-meals delivery service, go from couch potato to Ironman finisher, transform a life of suburban motherhood into a life of urban entrepreneurialism, leave a stable accounting job to nurse the ailing in overseas tent villages, and much more. The goals haven't just been about checking off bucket-list items; they've been about staking a claim on becoming someone bolder and more authentic, whether in the boardroom, on the world's biggest athletic stage, in their community, or in their private lives.

The number-one regret of those in hospice care is that they lived someone else's life, and not the one they felt they should have lived. We know from research that the main reason people don't pursue their most valued goals is fear—fear of everything from success, to change, to failure. And from where I sit and coach, the happiest people are those who take risks to be uncomfortable in the face of fear and find the grit to hang in there until they've given their goals every possible effort.

Grit is necessary across the lifespan

There's no question that grit has been established as an important strength in determining student outcomes; achieving excellence in rigorous settings, such as the military and elite athletic endeavors; and in professional settings, where maintaining focus and persistence during difficult times is the hallmark of inspirational leadership. But I believe we need grit no matter where we live, who we are, or what we want to do. We need to be resilient in overcoming addictive behaviors so that we can have happy lives. If we have children or loved ones with special needs, we need to be up to the challenge of the long-term, constant care and vigilance they require. We cannot shrink in the face of economic uncertainties, growing terrorism, and pervasive unhappiness. We must persevere if we are going to thrive, reinvent ourselves after midlife, and model courage for generations to come.

Given what I hear, both from clients and the feedback I get after my speeches, the problem isn't that people don't know that grit is important or don't want to be more emotionally resilient. The problem is that they just don't know how to do it and where to start. They don't know how to fight the tide of permissive parenting or the societal influences that lead to "good enough" standards. They don't know how to summon up enough willpower in a quick-fix, remote-controlled world, where everything is a click away and our attention span is now one second less than that of the average goldfish.[16] They also don't know that real science can assist them in changing their brains, their emotions, and their behaviors for the better. But if you are holding this book and you keep reading, you will soon know all of these things, and you will have the tools to change your life for the better.

"Don't ever, ever ring the bell"

In 2014, at the University of Texas at Austin commencement, Admiral William McRaven brought the house down with his inspirational eighteen-minute talk, "Ten Ways to Change the World." In it, he described the ordeals of SEAL trainees, including punishing runs in freezing cold weather, navigating underwater in pitch-black conditions, and being forced to do extra calisthenics after multi-hour endurance sessions. Admiral McRaven said if you want to change the world, you have to "sing when you are up to your neck in mud," "go down obstacles headfirst," and "punch the shark in the snout" when you are underwater, alone, and scared.[17] He finished his speech with the last of his ten change-the-world points, noting that everyone in SEAL training wants to quit at some point because they don't believe they have what it takes to persevere:

> Finally, in SEAL training there is a bell, a brass bell that hangs in the center of the compound for all the students to see. All you have to do to quit is ring the bell. Ring the bell and you no longer have to wake up at five o'clock. Ring the bell and you no longer have to do the freezing-cold swims. Ring the bell and you no longer have to do the runs, the obstacle course, the PT—and you no longer have to endure the hardships of training. Just ring the bell. If you want to change the world, don't ever, ever ring the bell.

If you want to learn how not to ring the bell, this book is for you, regardless of where you're starting in life or what you want to accomplish. The stories and research here will give you hope, confidence, and strategies to approach life in a new, more powerful way and to become your best and grittiest self. You will also see that when you get grit, you will inspire others to overcome obstacles, and that together we can bring the "awe" back into "awesome." Before we do that, though, let's take a look at how we got to this place, because if we understand how we got here and recognize how all of us may have played a role in reducing grit, then I believe we will be better equipped to turn it around and go in the right direction.

2

When Grit Is Gone

Wood Chips, Comfort Pigs, and Cuddlers

ver since I gave my TEDx talk in New York City in September
2014, my phone has been ringing off the hook. I have fielded
speaking requests from women's groups, corporations, hospitals, foreign governments, financial analysts, CEOs, universities, sports
teams, and Silicon Valley entrepreneurs, among many others, who want
me to come and talk to them and their peers about the importance of
grit and what people can do to develop it. I've been interviewed on radio
and television shows, from the United States to Australia, and wrote a
"Grow Your Grit" track for the website Happify. To help with the high
demand that shows no sign of letting up, I brought a manager on board
in 2015, and still, we can barely keep up with audiences around the
world who want to learn more about grit and how to build it.

Why is this? From the feedback I've received, I think people have
known for quite a few years that something is wrong in too many of
our families, schools, communities, and their companies, but until
they hear someone link the disparate elements all together, with relatable stories and research, it's difficult to make sense of what's happened
and understand how urgent the need is for change to occur before
it's too late. I believe this vague unease about what has happened to
parenting, academic standards, and some important cultural norms in
the last generation is part of what is fueling many Americans' discomfort with where our country is going, as well as their passion to effect
change in their own lives.

How did we get here? Why are companies hiring consultants to help
them cope with a generation of adults in which many need to be coached

on how to work hard, show up on time, be respectful, and have humility? Why do they feel like they need to step in and become the first to teach these young people how to set goals, be resilient, handle criticism well, and strive for excellence? Is it the fault of these Millennials? I think not. I think we have all played a role in creating a perfect storm that has lowered our national grit score, and I believe we all need to play a role in changing the standards and attitudes that have contributed to this decline.

"We hid the record board"

I'd like to start with one of my many stories of parenting from the "everyone's a winner" era that shows how nutty the self-esteem movement got for many parents in their desire to make their children feel special and happy at all costs. However, what's most instructive in this story is how the *kids* felt about removing high standards from their lives; it caused me to think more deeply about what many have been doing and why such an approach to parenting is so misguided.

In the late 1990s, when it was apparent that our oldest child, Haywood, was a talented swimmer, we joined a summer league team on the outskirts of Washington, DC, called Montgomery Square. The club came with an amazing legacy that we heard about almost immediately after we joined. Three men—Clay Britt, Dan Veatch, and Mike Barrowman—had emerged from the club's ranks in the late 1970s and early 1980s and gone on to national, world, and Olympic swimming fame. Mike Barrowman had even swum what USA Swimming called "the perfect race" when he won the 1992 Olympics in the 200-meter breaststroke, setting a world record that stood unchallenged for more than ten years.

When my husband and I heard about the club's unique history, we asked to see the record board so that we could marvel at how fast those swimmers had been when they were younger, and we knew our children would be interested, too. To our astonishment, we learned that the record board had been deliberately hidden in a back room. "It might discourage our kids if they see how fast those boys swam back then," a mother explained with a straight face. So instead of honoring and lifting up Britt, Veatch, and Barrowman as role models to emulate, including their work ethic, the parents had collectively determined that if their own children couldn't match the exploits of these remarkable swimmers, the kids would feel so bad about themselves that they might actually quit the team or, at the very least, lose faith in themselves.

Several years later, when I was a parent representative for the A team at the pool, I decided to do something about this ridiculous state of affairs. I commissioned the largest record board that had ever been made for a summer league team (at least, that's what I was told) and embedded in it pictures of our famous swimmers in their prime, along with descriptive write-ups of their swimming feats. Not only that, I flew all three swimmers back to Montgomery Square for a public dedication ceremony and swim clinic, both of which were mobbed by swimmers from dozens of clubs who all wanted to see these decorated athletes with their own eyes.[1]

Instead of being fazed by the times on the record board, I saw the opposite response. Every time an opposing team came to Montgomery Square for a swim meet, the first thing those kids did was cluster around the record board to see what the standards were so they could evaluate how fast they'd have to go to get their own names up there. The same was true with our own swimmers, who often stood and pointed at the times and the pictures after swim practices, possibly imagining themselves being up there one day, too.

My favorite story about the record board concerns a young man named Ben Gordon, who was fifteen when we first got the record board in 2003. I often saw him sit under an awning near the board, staring at it intently over the subsequent two years. Finally, a few months before his team participation was going to end because he was leaving for college, he approached me with his thoughts.

"Mrs. Miller, I think I can get one of those times," he said, pointing at the 100-meter backstroke time for boys between the ages of 15 and 18. The record was tough: it was held by Clay Britt, one of our record-board honorees, whose career had included being a world-record holder and the three-time NCAA champion in the 100-yard backstroke, but whose Olympic dreams had been quashed by the 1980 Olympic boycott.

Ben told me that he wanted to try to break the record at an upcoming home meet, which meant we'd need to have seven timers on his lane to make any record time as official as possible. Excited, I made the arrangements, and on the day of the meet I made sure I was the announcer so that I could play the *Rocky* theme song. When it was time, I told the crowd that Ben would be trying to break one of the oldest records on the board and that we all needed to cheer for him.

I still get goose bumps when I think about that morning. When Ben hopped into the water for the start of the race, hundreds of children and adults from both teams lined up along every spare inch of the poolside, screaming his name and clapping. As he churned through the water, the atmosphere was electric. And when his hand hit the wall at the finish, all of the timers punched their stopwatches and turned to one another to compare results. They broke into big smiles, because he'd broken the record by one-tenth of a second. Ben's reaction—a huge smile and joyous fist pump—was priceless, and the audience hooted and hollered for several long minutes to honor him and his gutsiness.

What is the moral of this story? That competition and high standards in our children's lives doesn't threaten them or make them unhappy, at least from what I've witnessed. On the contrary, having high standards, so that you know what elite performance is—which is what I think many people secretly long for—is what allows us to shoot for the stars, work hard, measure our progress, and evaluate where we stand. And when we work toward something that earns rightful recognition, like breaking a swim record, that's a moment of pride that means more than any of the false or easy praise some parents mistakenly think ought to take its place.

Winning! Easter eggs, fat rats, and color runs

One of the video clips that my audiences always love is from an April 2015 Easter-egg hunt in Sacramento, California, in which an attempt was made to break the world record for the largest Easter-egg hunt. In it, you can see some of the thousands of kids from around California who descended on the state capitol to vie for the half-million eggs containing money and special prizes that had been hidden around the grounds. The event immediately degenerated into chaos, as parents got into pushing and shoving matches with other adults—and even other children—to get the prizes.

"It was horrible," exclaimed frazzled mom Tessa Moon to a reporter. Clasping her children protectively, she said that adults had run rough-shod over two- and three-year-old kids, trying to snare as much booty for their children as possible.

This story isn't unusual, unfortunately. My files are bulging with story after story of parents shamelessly doing whatever they have to do to give their kids a win or an advantage, including breaking laws. The nicknames for parents like these, who try to remove all threatening competition from their children's lives, include "helicopter parents," "snowplow parents," and "lawnmower parents." These parents don't just stop at winning, though; they seek to remove all obstacles, hard-ship, and pain from their children's lives by making sure their kids never taste failure or disappointment. And if these parents don't get what they want, it's almost inevitable that a lawsuit will follow, or at least, threats of legal action.

This has played out in sports in troubling ways across several eco-nomic spectrums. Parents with the financial means have been known to sue teams and coaches when they don't think their children are get-ting sufficient playing time, and among less privileged communities there have been countless instances of coaches and parents and refer-ees settling grudges by getting into verbal altercations and fistfights, giving children an early look at how adult role models can behave when winning is all that matters. And some coaches have been caught telling their teams to throw matches to draw easier competition in later rounds, removing some of the most valuable life lessons that can come from sports, which include learning how to work hard for a dis-tant goal, be part of a cohesive team, always give your best effort, and win and lose graciously.

One of the most chronicled results of this kind of parenting and coaching is its "trophy culture," which was mocked in the 2004 film

Meet the Fockers, in which Ben Stiller's parents proudly show off one of his ninth-place ribbons to his fiancée's parents. The biggest beneficiary of this self-esteem movement has been the trophy industry, which has grown dramatically since the 1970s and now rakes in more than $3 billion annually. The losers of this movement, ironically, are the kids themselves, who have learned that showing up is all you need to do to be declared special.

And it hasn't just impacted their motivation; it has also changed the kids' brains, according to researchers, who say that being rewarded for doing nothing activates a "partial reward extinction effect" in the brain.[2] For example, rats who are given sugar water for simply standing in a maze and not solving it, or even moving at all, learn to simply sit and wait for the reward. Consequently, they plop down, get fat, and lose all curiosity about solving the maze. See any correlations here?

The fallout from over-rewarding athletic excellence might be even more dire than once thought. A much-discussed article in the *Wall Street Journal* lamented that the trophy culture had impacted the current generation of marathoners, who are forty-four minutes slower on average than previous generations.[3] U.S. running officials trace the problem to kids growing up seeing that the same reward happens whether you run for four seconds, four minutes, or four hours, reducing all incentive to learn how to work hard. Commenting on the ubiquitous celebrations runners have come to expect for just showing up, such as the popular Color Run, which is untimed and features runners being pelted with paint and glitter, one official lamented, "We don't have competitions anymore. We have parades!"

"It's the parents!"

This has also played out in academics, which I saw in my own elite girls' prep school in Washington, DC. The all-girl National Cathedral School, which has an enviable reputation of only taking a fraction of its applicants and then churning out intellectual young women who go on to some of the nation's most selective colleges, was where I spent nine happy years, soaking up a challenging education amidst high standards.

In the late 1990s, I presented on an alumnae panel about the process of getting a book published, and afterward I hung around for a while, enjoying the atmosphere and interacting with the students. Soon I found myself in a long marble hallway, strolling past ornate frames filled with the names of girls who had won some of the school's top awards over many decades in its annual Flag Day ceremony.

In a class of brilliant, diverse women, I'd been glad to get any kind of recognition on Flag Day, and I'd only earned one: a Bishop's Scholar award. Given to students who had not gotten below a B in all of their classes throughout high school, it wasn't one of the marquee awards, but it had meant something to me because it recognized general excellence. That afternoon, as I walked down the hallway looking at the Bishop's Scholar winners through the 1980s and beyond, the award list suddenly stopped. I looked up and down the corridor but didn't see it continuing elsewhere. Curious, I stuck my head into the headmistress's office to see if she was available and could tell me where it had gone.

"Aggie, where did the Bishop's Scholar award go?"

Aggie Underwood, the headmistress who had taken over after I graduated, was a no-nonsense woman, so I was glad I had caught her in a rare free moment. After hearing my question, she looked at me, smiled wearily, and then lowered her head to her desk and brought it back up with a resigned smile.

"Caroline, the difference between your time at this school and now is the parents," she said. "That award used to mean something, but we started to have parents calling us to say that their child couldn't get a grade below a B because it would hurt their college chances. They made it so hard for us not to give them the right grades that the number of kids winning the award just got bigger and bigger, until it became at least half the class. At that point, the award was completely meaningless, so we just discontinued it."

Although I'd heard about grade inflation and how consumers—the parents when it comes to most schools—made such kinds of demands, I'd naively thought it wouldn't touch a school like National Cathedral, which took so much pride in touting its rigor and high standards. But I was wrong, and I've continued to see this trend everywhere, with rare exception. In fact, one Ohio community named 222 high school graduating seniors as valedictorians in June 2015 because rampant grade inflation created so many "winners"![4]

Winning and giving kids what these adults think they "need," with or without the requisite effort, so that it's easier for the kids to keep racking up more achievements at the next level, has become so common that it's a surprise when you find an institution that doesn't do this. But it's exactly those types of places that provide the training and feedback that produce excellence and grit.

Antipathy toward real winners

When so many are declared "winners" and are accustomed to feeling special and being told how talented they are, it's become hard in some settings to recognize and reward genuine excellence. For example, the outpouring of hatred on social media for the most recent National Spelling Bee winners has been appalling. Instead of complimenting them on what Angela Duckworth's research has shown—that they studied more and worked harder than everyone else who didn't make the final rounds—a number of people charged that the Indian Americans are "stealing" the competition and that a "real American" child ought to have won.[5]

When they aren't derided, sometimes people who have achieved excellence are just ignored or marginalized. In 2016, one Texas public high school district refused to let graduating seniors wear the insignia of the National Honor Society to avoid "alienating" other students, while other schools are completely abolishing grades and valedictorians because "competition is unhealthy."[6] And my own children's high school, Bethesda-Chevy Chase High School, sitting smack-dab in the middle of the largest "super zip" in the country—that is, of wealthy and intelligent high achievers—decided to opt out of recognizing straight-A students at a quarterly-held donut break in 2016, partly because it encourages "competition" and creates "stress." The stress in this school district is apparently so "toxic" that the school board voted to abolish all senior final exams, in spite of the desires of the teachers, who felt it was the wrong move and would extinguish any reason for students to show up for class or try hard at the end of high school.

Who needs grades anyway?

One of the oddest trends that I witnessed as my children went through the school system wasn't just the pervasive grade inflation, but a bizarre variant: no grades at all. There is some irony in the concerns about the stress and workload students are expected to handle at school, because the current generation of students actually has less rigorous teaching and a smaller body of knowledge than previous generations, though students today think they're smarter. They also study much less than their parents did, mostly because of the innumerable distractions from television, technology, and smartphones.[7] But they expect good grades and believe simply showing up ought to get them at least a B.[8] Research shows that the average grade in the 1960s was a C, which was considered respectable, but now there is virtually no curve in most schools, including in the Ivy League, where schools like Harvard have an average grade of A-.[9]

Just as I imagine the teachers at my high school alma mater didn't agree with making sure many girls kept above-B averages to get the Bishop's Scholar award, regardless of the work they turned in, Harvard professors have found the elimination of the grade curve absurd and counterproductive to creating real scholars who can sift through conflicting information to come up with their own unique thoughts.[10] In an interview at Stanford's Hoover Institution, Harvey Mansfield, one of the longest tenured professors in Harvard's government department, revealed his contempt for the pressure he was under to give students the "right" GPA so that they could continue their march to elite graduate schools.[11] He described his own "ironic grading" process, a system he devised to ensure that students wouldn't fool themselves into believing they deserved a high grade when they hadn't actually earned it.

Here's how it works. At report-card time, Mansfield summons students to his office, where he sits them down and hands them a slip of paper with a letter grade. He tells them that the high grade is what he will be sending to the registrar's office for their official transcript. Then he hands them a second piece of paper with another letter grade. "This is the grade you deserve," he says. By all accounts, it's the second grade that matters to the students, because they—like all of us—know deep down when they haven't earned something.

Fake praise and an inflated transcript do nothing to help a person develop authentic self-confidence, but honest feedback and setting high goals do everything to help us understand where we stand and what we have to do to be really outstanding. If Mansfield gives a student a high grade on that second piece of paper, that is something they will always be proud of, because everyone knows ahead of time that tough, transparent standards were used to come up with evidence of actual success. Unlike becoming a high school valedictorian these days, which is so common it is akin to devalued currency, a high grade from Mansfield is rare, like finding a gold coin amidst a sea of pennies. Which one do you think carries more weight with students? Which approach would *you* choose if you wanted to develop authentic grit?

Although I have no doubt that students can and do take advantage of lax grading standards and easy As, as I know mine did from time to time, I'm not sure that this is what they really want or crave. In fact, there's evidence that students find their schoolwork too easy. For example, a biennial survey administered by the National Center for Education Statistics found that 37 percent of fourth graders felt their math wasn't challenging, and 51 percent of eighth-grade history students said their work is "often" or "always" too easy.[12]

I have never helped a single client cultivate grit by giving them empty praise or just taking their money while we engage in nice chats that don't include honest feedback about making progress toward their goals. We don't serve anyone well or help them fulfill their potential by propping them up, inflating their ego, avoiding difficult conversations, or refusing to ask hard questions. If we are never allowed to fail, how do we know if we are moving in the right direction? Taking away data that helps people adjust their efforts, evaluate their motives, and work harder is foolhardy and inconsistent with the pursuit of excellence and grit.

Bubble-wrapped teacups, snowflakes, and safe spaces

Although the parents of Millennials have come under intense scrutiny for raising "snowflakes" (beautiful and unique children that melt in the heat) and "teacups" (fragile and easily broken people), they certainly aren't the first to have lapses in parental judgment based on the popular "scientific" advice of the time. The Millennial generation does stand out, however, for being raised to see themselves as people who need to be saved from a scary world. This starts when they come home from the hospital to baby-proofed houses replete with outlet covers, cabinet locks, childproof lids, and door gates. They are chauffeured in cushioned splendor in cars and strollers, and everything they sit or lie on has to meet safety specifications. If they get to a playground—which may not happen because most children rarely venture far from their homes or yards, where vigilant parents and nannies stand guard—they are treated to more rounded plastic that does no harm, plus seatbelts on every swing.

We love our kids and are concerned about injury—and bad things can and do happen—but with that concern and our children's environments becoming "safer," we've overlooked the reality that developing grit involves learning how to take risks and even being exposed to unwanted illnesses and setbacks.[13] Too many Generation Xers and Millennials haven't benefitted from these hard knocks in the ways that previous generations did. They have gradually had familiar childhood games like tag and dodgeball, and activities like sledding, banned in their schools and communities because of the "danger" they present. Fewer are learning how to drive stick-shift cars or to parallel park because self-driving cars are removing the need to become competent at anything more difficult than steering a golf cart. And when they do go out, they are armed with cell phones that tell them where to go and how to get there. The phones can also send their every move back home to the computers of their helicopter parents.

Some parents' desire to protect their children from harm has gone from covering outlets to covering the eyes and ears of their preteens and teens so that they don't hear or see anything that might upset them.

This includes seeing real report cards, which one New York yeshiva for elementary school children suggested should only be done with "great discretion" because of the potential trauma that could occur if a child were to learn about critical comments or a bad grade. If the parents fear this outcome, the school offers to print a fake report card so that the child won't feel bad.[14]

Not only are real grades deemed too hard for some to take in, many elementary, middle, and high schools have acquiesced to a torrent of parental requests to ban books and topics they deem inappropriate for their children, including the *Adventures of Huckleberry Finn* and *Harry Potter and the Sorcerer's Stone*. These intellectually fragile teens then go to college, and if they feel "triggered" by a discussion that hurts their feelings, they lodge complaints against vulnerable professors and even fellow students about a so-called "microaggression," which results in black marks on students' records and busted careers among the professors who say their students "terrify" them.[15]

Speakers invited to universities are also being scuttled to avoid offending the sensibilities of those men and women who report feeling "unsafe" if a discussion or debate occurs anywhere within their vicinity. In fact, the month of May is now called "the season of dis-invitation" because so many commencement speakers (fifty-three in the last fifteen years) have been uninvited because of "comfort" issues. The uninvited include presidential historian Doris Kearns Goodwin, International Monetary Fund president Christine Lagarde, former U.S. Secretary of State Condoleezza Rice, and former U.S. Presidents George W. Bush and Barack Obama.[16]

One of the tributes paid to Supreme Court Justice Antonin Scalia when he passed away was that he always selected at least one law clerk who disagreed with him and would present opposing arguments for him to consider when writing his judicial opinions.[17] A cardinal sin of insecure leaders is that they surround themselves with yes-men, while self-confident, successful people like Scalia make sure they always hear differing points of view so that their final judgments are informed by as many facts as possible. If we are raising new generations to be incapable of hearing anything they don't already know and agree with, then we are ensuring that they will lack the confidence and humility to seek out data that will help them get better at whatever they want to do, which is a necessary component of grit.

There are so many stories about the out-of-control victimhood problem on campuses—alongside an alarming epidemic of crippling anxiety and depression—that it's hard to pick which ones best illustrate how this phenomenon has undermined the cultivation of grit to such a large extent.[18] Here are just a few that typify what is happening and that should give us all a disturbing lens into how our society increasingly discourages young adults from becoming emotionally resilient and able to learn from others who have dissenting viewpoints, while becoming more focused on their own feelings to the exclusion of others'.

"This is not a day care. This is a university!"

Several years ago, Brown University hosted a debate on the rape culture on campus, which led some students to protest that having two different viewpoints anywhere near them would cause them trauma. Brown's administration responded to the protesters by creating a "safe space" where students could come to feel protected from the dangerous conversations taking place within a mile of them. *The New York Times* wrote about this in an op-ed piece called "In College and Hiding from Scary Ideas," which noted that Brown's safe space that night hosted dozens of aggrieved students, who arrived to find a room with soft lighting, coloring books, chocolate-chip cookies, and video loops of frolicking puppies.[19]

Not every university takes the same timid approach as Brown with students who complain about feeling unsafe. In 2015, Oklahoma Wesleyan University president Everett Piper fired off an open letter to the entire school. He had given a Sunday-morning homily about love, and was approached afterward by an angry student who said that he and his peers deserved an apology because they had felt uncomfortable during the sermon. Why? They felt that if they didn't show love in the same way Dr. Piper's sermon suggested, it was a criticism of them. Instead of apologizing, Piper's public, pointed letter to faculty and students pushed back with his own criticisms of the pervasive culture of victimhood.

He wrote: "Our culture has actually taught our kids to be this self-absorbed and narcissistic! Any time their feelings are hurt, they are the victims! Anyone who dares challenge them, and thus makes them 'feel bad' about themselves, is a 'hater,' a 'bigot,' an 'oppressor,' and a 'victimizer.'" Piper ended with, "Oklahoma Wesleyan is not a 'safe place,' but rather a place to learn: to learn that life isn't about you, but about others; that the bad feeling you have while listening to a sermon is called guilt; that the way to address it is to repent of everything that's wrong with you rather than blame others for everything that's wrong with them. This is a place where you will quickly learn that you need to grow up! This is not a day care. This is a university!"[20]

Some alums are expressing their concerns about how their schools are conceding to such student demands by refusing to donate, saying it is "the only lever that can make a difference." Robert Longsworth, class of '99 at Amherst College and the seventh in his family to have attended the institution, told a reporter that he resigned as a class agent and president of the New York City alumni organization because of campus protests about removing the school's mascot and other issues, saying that Amherst was "so wrapped up in this politically charged mission rather than staying in its lane and being an institution of higher education."[21]

Other universities are drawing a line before new students even set foot on campus. In September 2016, the University of Chicago's college dean of students issued a welcome letter to freshmen that declared the university to be a space safe from safe spaces: "Our commitment to academic freedom means that we do not support so-called trigger warnings, we do not cancel invited speakers because their topics might prove controversial, and we do not condone the creation of intellectual 'safe spaces' where individuals can retreat from ideas and perspectives at odds with their own. . . . Diversity of opinion and background are a fundamental strength of our community. The members of our community must have the freedom to espouse and explore a wide range of ideas."[22]

We need more adults and institutions to hold the line in similar ways when challenged by youth who aren't fighting for a meaningful cause, but who are instead fighting to avoid hearing anything that pricks their conscience or causes them to think in intellectually critical ways. If we allow young people to wallow in self-absorption and woundedness, how will they ever get grit?

Can I bring my pig?

When all three of my children left home for college, they most wanted to stay in touch with our beloved standard schnauzer, Splash. Splash was central to their lives, as are many childhood pets. When they Skyped home, I had to put my laptop on the floor so that they could see and hear Splash. Our dog's passing at age 15 was easily the hardest thing they'd ever dealt with. I say this because I have tremendous empathy for students who want to bring their family pet to college, and there are definitely young adults with emotional challenges who require "comfort animals" because of their soothing presence. But like so many things that started with good intentions, the trend of bringing animals to college has only deepened this generation's inability to cope with the common everyday challenges young adults must face.

Two examples that capture the absurdity of the "comfort animal" situation involve pigs. A freshman arrived with her beloved 95-pound pig to Washington State University, but the pig was so scared of the freight elevator and stairs that it had to simply live around the clock with its owner on the second floor and defecate in a litter box. The other students began to complain that the pig smelled, chewed the carpet, and destroyed the furniture, but the university was helpless to do anything because of the Americans with Disabilities Act's requirement to provide accommodations for students claiming mental-health challenges. Ultimately, the college had to relocate the student to another dorm with a ramp for the pig, which was apparently less costly than fighting litigation.[23]

In a second circumstance, a twenty-nine-year-old woman carried an "emotional support" pig with her onto a crowded plane the day before Thanksgiving in 2014.[24] As startled passengers watched, the pig began to defecate on the floor and then howl when its owner tied it to an armrest and called it "a jerk." US Airways ultimately ushered the woman and her pig off the flight for being "disruptive," but they did so at the risk of facing a $150,000 fine from the U.S. Department of Transportation, which—like the colleges complying with the Americans with Disabilities Act—requires airlines to accommodate emotional-support animals because of the Air Carrier Access Act of 1986.

Pigs aren't even the most exotic animals popping up on planes, trains, and college campuses to help the rising number of anxious and depressed young adults cope with life. One well-circulated image on social media showed a turkey strapped into its own seat on a Delta flight. Passengers who followed the turkey through the airport said that it was even met by a wheelchair at the gate and then ushered through the terminal to general stares and public amazement.[25]

These and other examples show that it's woe to any passenger with feather or other types of allergies or issues who must contend with this new trend of traveling with comfort animals. A person who must have their way and insists upon making their comfort animal or fragility everyone else's problem isn't going to learn how to have authentic grit. In fact, refusing to acknowledge the importance of testing one's limits and foregoing familiar niceties to tackle a new stage of life is "stubborn grit." While certain people might actually need accommodations to get through life, more people need to think about whether they've allowed themselves to hold on to a "pacifier" for too long and whether it's time to test their inner strength.

Finally, this group of young adults with their comfort pigs, inflated grades, and fragile egos too often bring a sense of entitlement into the workplace, and the corporate world has had to sit up and pay attention. The Millennials are now the largest population in the workforce, so everyone is dealing with figuring out how to hire, train, and sometimes motivate the most promising candidates from this generation. Because too many Millennials don't work out, it's become a source of frustration for the people who do the hiring.

I often speak at conferences to human-resource professionals, who are responsible for hiring, training, and overseeing the culture in the organizations where they work. The lack of grit and how to deal with it is a hot topic among them. After I spoke to a Washington, DC, gathering of HR professionals, a middle-aged woman noted that she'd recently given a performance review to a thirty-something woman who burst into tears when she heard she had "met expectations." The HR professional shared with the audience that she'd come to realize that some Millennials equate "meets expectations" with a C grade, and that if they aren't informed that they "exceeded expectations," they feel like their world is coming to an end.

And when that happens, the Millennials have a new type of professional to turn to for comfort—a "cuddler." Cuddlers will "squeeze, tickle, and bear-hug" you in one of fifty nonsexual positions in at least sixteen states. Fees can start at $1 a minute, and go up to $425 for an overnight session.[26]

What the world needs now

When we look at the way in which many of the Millennials have been raised and acculturated, from the moment they entered the world to the moment they get their first job, it's easy to see why they wouldn't know much about grit—why it matters, what it gets you, or how to cultivate it. When you don't need to work hard to get rewards, your parents sweep away the world's difficulties, standards for excellence are reduced to mediocrity, and the working world provides you with perks like catered lunches and subsidized transportation, why shoot for the stars?

And if any of these young people do want to set and pursue difficult goals, where do they go to get the necessary skills if they've never had to do so before? How will they understand the importance of delayed gratification to build willpower? Who will be their role models? How will they learn to set goals and create accountability to stay on track, pivot, and keep going until the finish line? Who around them will be their contagious circle of support if so many are all in the same boat? And if they haven't had to hear or participate in difficult discussions about their performance or big ideas, how will they stretch their thinking to become innovative, creative, and proactive professionals?

When any of us build authentic grit, we create a foundation for a flourishing life. Let's learn more about it, then, as well as what we need to do to avoid falling into some of the damaging types of grit that won't benefit us or inspire others. And once we do that, we'll look at the individual components of authentic grit, which we can grow, use, and protect, as well as encourage in others—those with whom we live, work, and interact every day. Only then will we know that we won't "ever, ever have to ring that bell."

How Do You Start Getting More Grit?

to help you get more authentic grit, I want to take you through a process I've honed for twenty-plus years. I believe that the steps I take with my clients are the same steps you can use to your benefit. You might want to share this journey with an accountability buddy, a workplace friend, a mentor, or even a group—like a master-mind group—because you can't always see the progress you are making and it isn't easy to make yourself do difficult things when you're discouraged. However, when you know you have to report to someone else or you arrange to do things together, it's much easier to follow through.

What's your dream?

It all starts with a dream. People who come to me for help have a dream to go beyond their normal boundaries to do something that is significant and fulfilling, something they will regret not pursuing if they never make the attempt. These are sometimes people whom others would describe as successful, who don't necessarily have to change anything to have a comfortable existence for the rest of their lives, but who have a hunger to dig deeper and go further with a cherished goal—sometimes a hidden one.

My first question is simple and to the point: "What is the best possible outcome of our working together?" Just using the words "best" and "possible" awakens someone's senses to the idea that anything can happen, and that whatever that thing is, it can be magnificent. This is when people usually get right to the point and express some large, difficult goal: "I want to become an inspirational leader who helps other people find their purpose and bring it to work in a new way," "I want to stop waiting to be happy and start doing things that will make life more fulfilling," "I want to change my approach to work so that I can spend more time with my family and friends," or "I want to become an entrepreneur and control my own future."

I can usually tell when someone is passionate about what they want to do because they are very articulate about their goal—and the more they explain, the faster they talk. Because so much of what I do is over the phone, I have learned to "read" voices, and a passionate voice is warm, easy, and vibrant. People who are encouraged to share their dream without judgment will pick up steam as they describe their goal, usually because they have spent so much time in their heads thinking about it and trying to figure out how to make it happen.

My follow-up question is "So what then?" What I'm trying to get at with that question is what will change in the person's life once they accomplish that goal. The person who wants to learn how to sing and try out for shows like *American Idol or The Voice* might say that her family rained on her dream when she was a child and that she pushed it so far back she learned how to hide her true feelings about anything she cared about. Learning to sing would be a big step toward owning her own interests and goals, and because of the emotional hurdles to be overcome, simply taking voice lessons or trying out somewhere would represent monumental change for her.

"So what then?" also helps to elucidate how important the goal is to the person as opposed to anyone else close to them. If I hear the word "should," as in "I should go to medical school," that's a giveaway that the person might not have what we call "self-concordant" or "intrinsic" goals. Goals that matter to you and that will keep you in the game when it's challenging are goals that don't matter to anyone but you. If your dream is to please someone else, including your family or your coach, then it's not going to work out well.

What do you wake up for?

If it isn't already apparent, I like to ask people what they wake up for, or as the Japanese call it, their *ikigai,* which roughly translates as "that which I wake up for." In the process of discussing passion, one's purpose often emerges, but if it's not clear, I want to hear what pulls them forward. Purpose is never about doing something just for oneself. The happiest people feel like they do something that contributes to others, and that is what gives them passion.

Why is this the right time?

The saying "Timing is everything" is true when it comes to goals. Being ready to take risks, become uncomfortable, disrupt familiar activities, and break out of a safe space—either personal or professional—will require all of the ingredients we see in grit, including passion and persistence. I don't want to work with people who are half-hearted or unsure about chasing their dream because it will be frustrating for both of us if we begin to work together and the first speed bump makes them quit in self-doubt.

I've noticed that there are several important times in a person's life when one can take advantage of biology and natural transitions to take a leap into the unknown. Many people come to me when they have become complacent about life and want to see if they can find more excitement by pursuing a dream. Other people use the empty nest or a critical birthday—forty, fifty, sixty, etc.—because it suddenly strikes them that life is moving forward at a rapid pace, and they didn't realize that they were stuck or unfulfilled until the milestone rolled around; psychologists have dubbed this the "fresh start effect."[1] Another important time for risk-taking is when someone hasn't found success with something else—a relationship or a job, for example—and they feel like they have nothing to lose. J.K. Rowling is a famous example of this. In her commencement speech at Harvard University in 2008, she said she wrote the Harry Potter series because "I had nothing left to fail at."

When I ask about the timing, I also find out whether this is something the person has attempted before, but not achieved. If someone has an unfulfilled urge from a previous miss, I know that it's a dream that won't leave them alone and that giving it their best shot is a piece of how they wish to remember themselves. Diana Nyad, the endurance swimmer who tried and failed to swim from Cuba to Key West, Florida, in her late twenties, gave up on her dream until it returned full force in her late fifties. She later shared the story in a speech. The question she asked herself as she approached the age of sixty with the swim still haunting her was, "Who do you want to be, not what do you want to do?" People who have pursued a goal before have experience that they have learned from, experience that will help them craft new strategies for overcoming challenges. That tells me that they are also resilient and have the humility to try again at something that has defeated them.

What's the hardest thing you've ever done?

I like open-ended questions that get to the heart of what I need to know about someone, and one of the things I need to understand most is someone's appetite for doing difficult things. You might think that many who are successful in life have overcome self-imposed challenges, but I've learned repeatedly that this isn't true. I have lost count of how often I've asked people this question and they've answered, "I've never really done anything hard." That answer is exactly why they hire a coach like me. They have succeeded in spite of never going outside their comfort zone, and they have become so accustomed to doing well that they don't know how they'd cope with the risk of failing—or actually failing!—at something.

As we get older, it becomes more difficult to stick our necks out and take a risk, which is why I think so many people at midlife struggle with depression and ennui. A friend of mine lost her college-age daughter in a freak amusement-park accident when she was in her forties, and that was when she realized how many people in her peer group were living dull and uneventful lives, people who thought taking a risk meant trying a new restaurant. Determined to live life to its fullest, and partly in tribute to her daughter, too, my friend joined a mastermind group and changed her professional and personal life. It was challenging but exhilarating, and she says that in the face of such darkness, finding new outlets for passion and growth literally saved her life when she wasn't sure she wanted to be alive.

When someone tells me that they don't have a history of doing tough things outside their comfort zone, I have them take Angela Duckworth's Grit Scale to determine where they stack up in the grit department. I've found the test to be remarkably revealing about how someone perceives their appetite for hard work, and if the score is low—3 or below—it's usually because they have a history of running from new things or avoiding challenges. For some, their interests are so varied that they just disengage from projects the moment something new comes along, while others set goals they know they'll achieve without too much effort or risk.

For people who want to set the bar high, grit is an essential character strength, and when I coach someone who doesn't have it, I tell them that if they want to work with me, they'll need to do things they have never done before, like say no to temptation and yes to constructive feedback. And when someone is ready for that challenge, it is a wonderful ride for both of us.

Who wants you to succeed?

This might be the most important question I ask people when assessing their likelihood for success. I know from experience and research that you can have a passion and be hardworking, curious, and hopeful, but if you are surrounded by people who don't want you to succeed or who are ambivalent about any changes you want to make, then some of our work together will need to include a clear-eyed assessment of what I call your "web of influence."

People who succeed at long-term goals never succeed alone. They build and nurture relationships around them that provide support, advice, and accountability. Without that supportive network, they'd never be able to regroup during difficult times and find the will to keep going. In a technologically driven society, when it's easier to text someone than look them in the eyes, some people have let important relationships lapse or haven't ever confessed their fears or goals to anyone who might be able to help them.

What are your top strengths?

Every single client who enters my practice takes the Values in Action (VIA) Character Strengths Survey right away. I love this survey because it makes sense to me. I find it to be affirming and accurate, and when I go through the results with clients, they see themselves in new and positive ways. I admit that I'm biased because Marty Seligman and Chris Peterson were my primary mentors, and they coauthored the survey. But I've also found that it is more useful to me than any other strengths survey I've encountered, my clients prefer it because it is so easy to understand, and it is an essential source of information for anyone who wants to understand their strengths and weaknesses, particularly when it comes to the cultivation of grit.

Some of the top findings from researchers who study the results of the VIA among different cultures and age groups are that people who identify and use their top five strengths in positive ways throughout the day are happier and more successful in the pursuit of their goals.[2] It has also been found that people who deliberately "own" their top strengths and interact with others through the prism of those strengths come across as more "authentic" to other people, making it easier to be around them.

When people seek to get grittier, there are several qualities that I look for when I first scan their test results, which rank their strengths from 1 to 24. Among the ones that I know will be important for grit are self-regulation, sense of purpose, hope, zest, humility, and bravery. I'm never surprised when people's bravery and self-regulation are low, because it usually indicates that they don't have good impulse control and have trouble pushing themselves out of their comfort zone, which is exactly why they want to work with a coach. If purpose, hope, and zest are low, I find that the process of exploring someone's passions and then identifying a strategy to help them achieve goals that align with their purpose gets the needle unstuck.

Another important conversation that I have with clients is around the overuse and underuse of their top strengths. While strengths are good, the overuse or underuse of those same strengths can often get them into trouble, preventing them from having the right kind of grit for the right goals. One example is kindness: when people overuse their kindness, they can be taken advantage of by "takers," thus preventing them from attending to their own needs and desires. Another example is perseverance: when people overuse it, they feel the need to finish everything they start, and such doggedness isn't always in their best interests. I call that "stubborn grit."

The final reason I start all engagements with the VIA is that it's been found to boost well-being, and people who want to be persistent in goal pursuit will need to have a flourishing outlook on life if they are going to persist in hard times, handle stress with humor and resilience, and put their best foot forward whenever possible.

When are you at your best?

Building on the VIA, I ask all of my clients to write an essay called "Me at My Best." This was our first assignment at Penn in the MAPP program, and it had a profound impact on me. In this essay, you write about a time when all of your top five strengths were used in a transformational moment or a time in your life when you were "at your best." This can be a personal experience, a professional experience, or both. The idea is to find a time or times when your strengths came out in the right way and at the right time to create a positive outcome. This might be a time when you made a difference in someone else's life, when you achieved something important for yourself, or when you were going through a tough period that was made easier because you leaned on those strengths to survive and thrive.

This essay is usually an aha! moment for people for several reasons. The first is that many of us take our strengths for granted and don't realize that how we see the world isn't how everyone else sees it. For example, people who have curiosity in their top five strengths are accustomed to asking questions and being open to new experiences. They can't comprehend why other people wouldn't do the same. Understanding that their curiosity is something that brings them benefits and shapes how they interact with others becomes a powerful tool they can use to understand themselves and craft strategies to help them do hard things.

My own essay was illuminating. My top five strengths are love, creativity, zest, bravery, and wisdom, and my initial reaction when I saw them was puzzlement. It just seemed obvious to me that people would be creative if they wanted to have interesting lives or make new connections in their heads to solve problems, so I didn't think of it as a strength—I took it for granted that everyone else must have it. Taking one's strengths for granted and assuming that they aren't anything special is very common, but I didn't yet know that. I also didn't really understand why wisdom would be there. Wisdom about what? I wondered.

And then it hit me. I had drawn upon all of those strengths when I wrote about my recovery from bulimia in *My Name Is Caroline.* I had used love to care enough about myself to work on getting better, and I had to love others in order to want to share that story. I needed to have creativity to write the book, and zest was the life force that I drew upon to give me energy when I wanted to quit. Bravery was something that felt natural to me when it came to deciding to write the book at a time when almost no one was talking publicly about bulimia. Even if I didn't see my action as particularly brave, I felt it was important to speak out. And wisdom came from being on the other side of the eating disorder, sharing my strength and hope with others so that they could continue to fight for themselves, too.

For anyone who wants to develop grit, knowing when you are at your best is essential because those vignettes provide a blueprint of how you can use your strengths in the right context and the right dose to do something well. For example, if bravery is a top strength, but you use it in reckless ways that hurt you, doing this exercise will show you a time when you were effectively courageous and remind you of how to be that person again. The more you remember to think about the best ways to use your strengths when they emerge, the more likely you'll be to use them to serve yourself and others in positive ways. And here's one fascinating tip: a sure sign that you have a top-five strength is when you are more offended by its absence in others than might be common.

Who is your best possible future self?

An elegant writing exercise called "Best Possible Future Self" is very powerful in a number of ways when it comes to revving up the engine of happiness and fueling the energy for goal pursuit. It is deceptively simple: people write about their life ten years from now as if everything has gone as well as possible and their dreams have become a reality. There are many reasons why this is an essential step to take on the road to cultivating grit. The first is that this exercise unlocks a vision of who you want to become, and it's ten years in the future, which is a wonderful time frame for contemplating the fruits of long-term labor. So, if you haven't yet envisioned what your life can be like if you accomplish your biggest goals, this exercise forces you to go there. It also helps you reprioritize your life, because many of us carry around different ambitions, but we don't realize that pursuing one of them will make it impossible to accomplish another important goal. Seeing the classic situation of "goals in conflict" and choosing to make one of them more important frees up energy that is necessary for grit.

This writing exercise is also valuable because it puts you in touch with who you want to be in the future. It's been found to induce more compassion for your older self, leading some to even save more money for retirement! It also generates more hope and optimism for your future, which are essential mind-sets for grit as well.[3] Finally, by going into the future and then coming back to the present, and doing it in that order, you set up a situation called "mental contrasting." It's been found that when we visualize our ideal future and then bring ourselves back to the present to contemplate whatever obstacles stand in our way, we are more zestful and committed to taking first steps than if we start with where we are today and think about what has to happen to make our future dreams a reality, which can feel overwhelming at first.[4]

What obstacles will you have to overcome?

Once my clients have gotten their VIA strengths, pondered their purpose, explored their web of influence, examined their "Me at My Best" story, and written their "Best Possible Future Self" essay, we are well on our way to evaluating whether they have the grit they need to succeed, and what we will need to do to get more. At this point, we talk about potential obstacles and what types of unexpected setbacks might come their way. If someone has tried to accomplish a goal before, then they have a good idea where they could get tripped up, so we talk about how they handled those setbacks and what they can do differently this time, including finding role models who have weathered similar setbacks and rebounded.

This can result in someone coming up with a new "story" about their life, according to research on narrative journaling and expressive writing. The *Journal of Personality and Social Psychology* published a study that found students who were exposed to stories of others' struggles were moved to write new narratives of their own lives, reframing challenges as positive opportunities for growth. When compared to a control group, the group that rewrote their personal stories was far less likely to drop out of college. These results have been replicated with other groups, including married couples who wrote about their conflicts from the perspective of a neutral third party. "These writing interventions can really nudge people from a self-defeating way of thinking into a more optimistic cycle that reinforces itself," said Timothy D. Wilson, a University of Virginia psychology professor and researcher.[5]

Now what?

Once my clients have explored their purpose, identified their strengths, created long-term goals, and made a commitment to move forward with the help of my coaching, then we dig in. We set up a timeline for completion, devise a system of accountability, determine the frequency of our calls, and settle on which metrics we'll use to determine how progress is being made. And woven into all of our work are discussions of what it will take to not quit when progress falters, mood dips, life throws curveballs, and motivation wavers. Since the quality of grit will largely determine whether all of the other work will even matter or pay off, let's take a look at the type of grit I've found to produce the best outcomes and to actually benefit everyone else, too: authentic grit.

And while we do that, as we delve further into learning about the different kinds of grit, and how to cultivate what I call "authentic grit," I'd like you to get started on your own answers to the questions I've shared in this chapter. Take the time to ponder, reflect, and write down what comes up for you.

- What is the dream (or dreams) you want to pursue, and that you know you'll regret not pursuing if you don't get started?

- What do you wake up for?

- Why is this the right time to go outside your comfort zone?

- What's the hardest thing you've ever done?

- How did you succeed at that hard thing?

- Who wants you to succeed?

- What are your top strengths? You can take the free Values in Action Character Strengths Survey at viacharacter.org, where you will find a link to the survey. The assessment takes about fifteen minutes to complete, and you'll be provided with the results.

- When are you at your best, and how do your strengths emerge in those situations?

- Who is your best possible future self?

- What obstacles will you have to overcome to live your best possible life?

While you're working on your own assessment, let's continue as well with a closer look at the different kinds of grit.

4

Authentic Grit

What Is It?

f someone like Adolf Hitler fits the definition of grit, how could it be a good thing?" This is usually the first question I get asked when I speak to audiences about grit. The moment people understand how passion, hard work, and dedication to a goal fit into a traditional description of grit, they usually think of someone they know who fits the definition in a good way, like Gandhi or someone in their extended family who showed them early that work pays off. But it isn't long before they get a puzzled look and ask about Hitler.

Undoubtedly, this has crossed your mind, too. You might know someone who has modeled change and passion as they've made a positive difference in other people's lives, but you can probably also think of someone who became obsessed with achieving a certain kind of success, and whose drive or actions did more harm than good, and possibly didn't even bring them joy. You might even know people who have exhibited both good and bad sides of grit at different times, which might lead to confusion about how to know when you are using it well and when you need to be careful not to head in the wrong direction.

Suzanne's story: same person, different uses of grit

A client of mine—let's call her Suzanne—was a good example of someone who veered in the wrong direction because of grit. She was a model hard worker, and her character strengths ranked her very high in qualities like love of learning, self-regulation, and perseverance. She hired me because she had a dream of becoming a novelist, but she found herself mired in unsatisfying professional work that helped pay the bills yet brought her no satisfaction. She also rattled off a long list of obligations that cluttered her days: carpools, cooking, hospitality stints at her church, and much more. She told me that because of her work ethic and attention to detail, she was usually the first one tapped to head a committee, run a meeting, or organize a potluck, all of which offers she accepted. And although part of her longed to say "no" to many of these requests, once she was goaded into a "yes," she saw things through to completion, regardless of the obstacles.

Suzanne clearly had grit, but it wasn't bringing her any joy because she was using it to plod through life on other people's terms, and almost never in ways that lit her up. I asked her about a time when she had used that same discipline and attention to detail to do something that made her happy, and she had to think back to more than twenty years earlier, to a time before she was married.

As she described it, just out of college she'd been accepted to a master's program in creative writing, and instead of taking a "safe" job like her parents wanted, she'd pursued the craft of writing and had gotten odd jobs in the television industry, even writing for one of the late-night comedy shows. It had been hard but rewarding work, and she'd been exhilarated by how she spent her days, the quality of the people who surrounded her, and the "wins" she'd had when some of her work got published. Money had been tight, but she'd felt in flow every day. She never even complained about the constant rejections from literary magazines because she felt like she was learning things that would help her become a better writer in the future.

After getting married and moving for her husband's career, Suzanne put her own dreams on hold, doing whatever needed to be done as her family grew. Instead of pursuing her own goals, she had grit for other people's goals—her community, her children, her husband, and her friends. By the time she reached me, she was drained, dispirited, and counting the days until her children left for college. Brushing off her old longings, reconnecting with her passions, choosing to disengage from unnecessary obligations, and using her focus and work ethic to write again was exactly what she needed. Instead of using her grit to get to the finish line of goals she didn't feel passionately invested in, Suzanne used those same skills to return to writing in her free time, with the goal of finding an agent and eventually publishing a novel. And with that, she brought life back into her life.

Tiger Woods and Casey Martin

The stories of pro golfers Casey Martin and Tiger Woods further demonstrate how grit can be both positive and negative. Let's take a look at each. Woods is one of the most famous and celebrated golfers of all time. He has had to work very hard and through many injuries to continue to be relevant in the golfing world. Woods set the world on fire as a youngster, at Stanford, and then as a professional golfer, establishing new standards for the sport and drawing huge crowds and television ratings because of his exciting and passionate style of play.

There's no question that he has grit, but is it the type you want to emulate? While legendary for his sporting feats, he hasn't distinguished himself as a good role model in the way he treats women or in the way he handles himself on the golf course when he is angry or frustrated. His icy, unfriendly demeanor during press conferences is well documented, and he has had numerous fallings-out with caddies, coaches, and other professional golfers. People might respect his talent, but they don't always like or respect his behavior. One ESPN commentator mused that Tiger may have been groomed to be a winner by his doting parents, but not necessarily "an overcomer," because he hasn't found his mental and physical stride since the fateful 2008 night when his then-wife confronted him about his extramarital escapades and bashed his car with one of his golf clubs.

On the other hand, Casey Martin, a former teammate of Woods at Stanford, has the type of grit that uplifts and inspires others. Martin—called "the Jackie Robinson of golf"—suffers from Klippel-Trenaunay syndrome, a birth defect that will eventually cost him his right leg. He walks with a marked limp, and as a result, was allowed to use a cart in NCAA tournaments at Stanford. After he graduated, however, the Professional Golf Association refused to allow him to use a cart, arguing that tournaments are "private" and thus not subject to accommodations through the Americans with Disabilities Act. Refusing to bow to discrimination, Martin won his lawsuit against the PGA, kept playing and coaching, and made the US Open cut in 2012—after years of middling-to-poor scores, once even losing his tour card. Despite setbacks, his love for the game remains unshakeable, and it's something he shares with his students at the University of Oregon, where he is the golf coach. This type of passionate pursuit of a goal in the absence of worldwide stardom and mixed with setbacks, graciousness in defeat, humility, and an unwavering refusal to quit is the type of authentic grit we want to cultivate.

How can you get on the right grit track?

The little blue engine, the heroine of the popular children's book *The Little Engine That Could,* has the first ingredient of grit. She starts on the same life track as everyone else, but as she goes on the journey of her life, she finds obstacles and wants to quit. Life is too hard. But she eventually summons up the will and energy to tow a bunch of train cars up an enormous hill, saying, "I think I can—I think I can—I think I can." As appealing as this tale has been for generations of children who learn about confidence and hard work from the narrative, if you aren't careful, you can become the engine that goes off on a variety of tracks that might look appealing, but that won't take you to happy places. For example, you can be so tough and persistent that you fail to heed the signs and warnings that you are cultivating "stubborn grit."

You can also become so addicted to the goal of winning at all costs that you take shortcuts and cheat. I call this "faux grit." And what if you are a disciplined, dedicated, goal-driven person, but you fail to acknowledge the help of others and feel the need to relentlessly trumpet your successes? Is this the type of grit that fosters harmony and excellence in a family or an organization? I think not, so I call this "selfie grit." Grit without leavening character strengths and positive purpose only results in a busy and often-unrewarding existence.

How does authentic grit differ from other kinds of grit?

To qualify for the label of authentic grit, it's not enough to be resilient, persistent, and passionate. I believe that gritty behavior is a positive force only when it awes and inspires others to want to become better people and imagine greater possibilities for themselves. People who display it make us wonder, "What if I went after hard things, too? What if I devoted energy and time to cultivating my passions? What if?"

I believe I'm alive because another woman had the courage to demonstrate authentic grit in my presence at the right time, in the right way, and when I was most receptive to hearing it. In early 1984, I was at a twelve-step meeting for compulsive eaters when a tall, blonde woman shared the story of her eating disorder and said, "I'm recovering from bulimia one day at a time." Because it was so rare to hear people talk about eating disorders without shame, or to have anything to offer in the way of hope, this woman's presence in a church on a cold winter night lit me up and changed me forever. My passion to be alive had been reduced to a flicker for years, but this woman's words turned it into a fire that still burns. I'll never stop being grateful to her. What if she had decided to keep her story to herself or had thrown in the towel on recovery because it was too difficult? What if she hadn't had the humility to learn from her own setbacks and persevere, or didn't want to help others?

I believe I was meant to be sitting in that room in enough despair that I recognized a lifeline when I saw it. I've always felt that something bigger than me—God, a higher power, a universal force that wants all of us to be healthy—guided me to be there that night, and that because I had the gift of writing, my purpose emerged and gave my life meaning. I suddenly knew that if I could muster the same zest, discipline, optimism, and kindness as the woman sitting in front of me, I could tell my own story of recovery in a book that might reach thousands of people who needed the message. And if that happened, I would leave the world better than it had been before. So that's how I started my own journey to authentic grit—in a place of darkness, but one that was perfect because it provided the right impetus to change for the better.

Positive relationships with others

One of the first signs of authentic grit is embodied in the story I just shared about hearing a story of recovery when I needed it most. The people who have the quality that makes such a positive difference pull us into their lives in uplifting ways, and they are inclusive, not exclusive. They flourish in their relationships and build other people up. People with authentic grit foster teamwork and camaraderie. Authentic grit is magnetic, and you want to associate yourself with someone who is passionate about something in life because you want to feel that way, too.

The same passion that those with authentic grit bring to goal pursuit is what allows them to create deep connections with others. They are people who don't just love and appreciate others but also are comfortable being loved and appreciated. It's interesting to note that the most beloved Hollywood movies are never about succeeding at a big goal and celebrating alone; they are about being gritty and sharing the journey with loved ones, win or lose.[1]

The wrong kind of grit often celebrates alone. In fact, this was the poignant message of the book—later turned into a movie—*Into the Wild.* Christopher McCandless mistakenly thinks that being isolated and self-reliant is the epitome of happiness, but he dies alone in agony, after eating poisonous berries, in a frigid school bus in Alaska. The last words he penned in the margins of a book that was later found simply read, "Happiness is best when shared."

High in hope

People with authentic grit are hopeful and optimistic. Although they may not always be correct about what they think they can do, their positive beliefs offer protective benefits. People with this outlook work longer and harder than others and are less likely to quit when challenged. A hopeful mind-set also allows people to generate more potential solutions for accomplishing their goals and makes them believe they can carry out those solutions, too. But hope and optimism are hard to sustain when you aren't pursuing your own goals and are trying instead to please others or achieve something that is more superficial than significant.

Humility

Authentic grit is also marked by humility, which never promotes itself but rather attracts others. This is the humility of heroism under fire—for example, some selfless act that you don't learn about until the person passes away. It is the humility of the woman who has toiled in obscurity for years without trumpeting her work improving the lives of others in a community food bank, proud because she knows she is giving her best to a meaningful goal that matters to her. Authentic grit is strikingly devoid of narcissism and the need to be recognized for what one does. Quite the contrary—those with authentic grit know what matters, and don't need anyone's approval or praise, nor do they seek publicity to boost their confidence or self-esteem.

Self-confidence

Authentic grit is characterized by genuine confidence. People with authentic grit bet on themselves because they know they will have toxic regrets if they don't give their goals everything they have. Their countenance can be unassuming, but they have a determined mind-set that is known to the people around them. The person with authentic grit exhibits grace under pressure, as well as in defeat, and is consistent in his or her unwillingness to quit, whether a trophy or public acclaim or even no reward at all awaits at the finish line. Because they have faith in their abilities and a willingness to learn from mistakes, they have a battle-hardened confidence that is also spotted in the best leaders.

Givers, not takers

Authentic grit is also defined by being the right kind of giver. These men and women don't give to their own detriment. They primarily surround themselves with those who share their mind-set but are not above mentoring others who lack focus or discipline. They recognize that being generative and seeing the lights go on in others' eyes is part of a positive legacy, so they give without strings attached, and often do so secretly and without fanfare. So while people with authentic grit are selfish with their time and energy when they have to be, it's never just all about them, because they know that other people matter.

Appropriate focus

Authentic grit is focused. People who have this quality aren't dogged finishers in everything in life. In fact, every person I interviewed who fit my criteria for authentic grit laughed immediately and said "No!" when I asked them if they are gritty in every area of life. They preserve their self-regulation for what really matters, and don't waste time on everything that crosses their path. They narrow down what is meaningful to them and have no trouble finishing last in something else or being self-deprecating about something they aren't good at.

Bob Vallerand, a world-renowned expert and researcher on passion, says that this distinction is also made between having "harmonious" and "obsessive" passion. People who are harmoniously passionate can find enjoyment both inside and outside of their primary goals, while obsessively passionate people can rarely let go of being winners. It was often said about fallen bicyclist Lance Armstrong that he could never lose at anything, whether it was a lawsuit or a triathlon. His passion to be the best was a toxic obsession that hurt others, and not just him.

Stubbornness

Authentically gritty people have a certain kind of stubbornness, but use it as a form of "alternate rebellion" because it's more effective than just being a disruptive troublemaker, which some of them—like Louis Zamperini, the real-life hero from the 2014 film *Unbroken*—have admitted to being before latching onto a focus that gave their lives purpose and meaning. As a young man, Zamperini ran away from home regularly, stole, fought, and was constantly in trouble until he discovered his talent for running, which he tirelessly honed until he reached the Olympics, finishing in eighth place in the 5000-meter race in 1936. Authentically gritty people can be obstinate, defiant, rebellious, and feisty, but they put that energy to good use when they need to dig deeper for positive goals.

Learn from failure

People with authentic grit have experienced disappointment in their goal pursuit, and as a result, they've had to learn how to handle defeat, integrate its lessons, and continue on their path. Cam Newton, quarterback of the Carolina Panthers NFL team, needed grit to overcome his humble beginnings and achieve college-football stardom; he even won the hearts of Carolina fans during his epic 2015 season of near-perfection. But after the Panthers' loss to the Denver Broncos at Super Bowl 50 in February 2016, he pouted at the post-game press conference, abruptly walking out after two minutes with his sweatshirt pulled over his head.

In stark contrast, his teammate Josh Norman, a cornerback who received no Division I scholarship offers in spite of a stellar high school career and had to walk on to a relatively obscure college team to get a shot at playing, was the classier person. This was undoubtedly because he had been humbled repeatedly in life as he tried to achieve his goals and understood that true greatness means knowing how to handle both success and defeat, extracting the best from each experience. As the 2016 Super Bowl ended with his team booking the loss, Norman made a point of publicly saluting Peyton Manning, the opposing quarterback, in the waning moments of the game. He could have walked off the field in disappointment, but he chose to pay homage to Manning's long, storied career instead of focusing only on himself.

Authenticity

People with authentic grit are comfortable in their own skin. When you meet them, you may not detect special airs, and they are as comfortable being with other people as they are being alone. When they do the difficult, deliberate work that usually accompanies long-term goals, they do it alone and without excuses. They are not perfectionists to such an extreme that they beat themselves up, though. They know when to have enough self-compassion and wisdom to step away, regroup, refocus, and then return to action.

The Values in Action Institute in Cincinnati, Ohio, which is devoted to the study of character strengths, has actually found that people who use their top strengths in pursuit of their goals don't just succeed more often, but also that *other* people are comfortable in their presence because of their authenticity. They don't try to be someone they are not but have found instead that accepting who they are and using their talents in the best ways for the best outcomes doesn't just serve them well, it also helps them in their relationships with others, too.

Growth mind-set

Finally, people with authentic grit have what is called a "growth mind-set" and not a "fixed mind-set." People with a growth mind-set believe that hard work is the key to succeeding, and their curiosity and willingness to take risks allow them to explore different approaches and be flexible in goal pursuit. A fixed mind-set believes that intelligence and talent are finite predictors of success and that getting a quick win is more important than working toward an important outcome. The fixed mind-set also believes that effortless winning is most important, rather than being someone who grinds away toward success, dismissing the idea of doing hard work because it is something that only less talented people have to do.

Can everyone develop authentic grit?

Authentic grit isn't something that is reserved for only a few special people, nor are those who have earned that classification clearly destined from childhood to be tough, resilient, and awe-inspiring. While Angela Duckworth's research has found that some of the strengths that undergird grit, such as optimism and impulse control, are hardwired at birth, many of the traits and behaviors of authentic grit can be learned. For example, goal-setting is a learnable science, as is self-regulation, even if some are born with a jump on it. Humility is also a chosen behavior, and learning how to make friends and build positive relationships is the subject of one of the best-selling books of all time: Dale Carnegie's classic *How to Win Friends & Influence People.* I would not have written this book if I were just describing an elite group of winners we could never aspire to emulate. But before we roll up our sleeves to begin working on developing more of the right kind of grit in our lives, let's get clear about the differences between "good grit" and "bad grit."

Good Grit

Mt. Rushmore, Mt. Olympus, Celebrity, and Ordinary

I n order to make it easier to understand the differences between good grit and bad grit, I've divided up the types of positive authentic grit that I see in the world, along with examples to help flesh out their significance and meaning. I will explain why each type is important and how we can benefit from identifying, studying, and emulating its finest features. In the next chapter, I will tackle the grit approaches that aren't quite as positive, along with warnings about how to avoid taking the strength of follow-through and turning it into a weapon you can use against yourself or others.

Mt. Rushmore grit

When I evaluated a number of great figures from history and pondered how to best describe their brand of grit, I discovered that they share some important characteristics that set them apart in noteworthy ways. These men and women are the ones who were lit up by a cause they felt passionate about and who reflected universally admired values like fairness, justice, and love. In their journey to accomplish something significant and historic, they overcame numerous obstacles—some life threatening—but never backed down for long because of fear, despair, or loss. Their behavior was also unique for its unusual display of dignity and self-regulation. They controlled their reactions to hate, envy, or aggression directed at them from others, and in so doing, became leaders who changed the course of history and attracted followers who admired and embraced their cause, and helped change the world for the better.

I call these men and women possessors of "Mt. Rushmore grit" because like the granite landmark in the Black Hills of South Dakota that features the faces of four of the greatest American presidents—George Washington, Abraham Lincoln, Theodore Roosevelt, and Thomas Jefferson—their deeds changed the course of history and have become enshrined in the hearts and minds of generations of grateful men and women. They include people like Jesus of Nazareth, Mahatma Gandhi, Martin Luther King Jr., Harriet Tubman, Susan B. Anthony, and Bill Wilson, the cofounder of Alcoholics Anonymous. All of them opposed actions that represented the worst of man's behavior—hatred, colonialism, racism, sexism, and alcoholism, to name just a few—and put their own reputation, health, and safety at risk to do so. Their ability to hold fast to their ideals and goals in spite of hardship, condemnation, and abuse is why we live in a freer, safer, and better world today. Where would we all be if they hadn't had this particular brand of authentic grit?

We can see Mt. Rushmore grit in our daily media as well. For example, Malala Yousafzai, a Pakistani advocate for female education and the youngest Nobel Prize winner ever, was shot in the face in 2012 by the Taliban because of her belief that girls deserve the right to be educated. Her articulateness, miraculous survival, poise, and subsequent refusal to abandon her cause out of fear, despite death threats, is one of the most inspiring examples of courage and grace under fire I've ever encountered—and I've seen many men and women grow respectfully silent in person and in the media when her name comes up. If you've heard her story, it has left its fingerprints on your soul, too.

Another example of Mt. Rushmore grit is Sandy Grimes, a CIA officer who watched helplessly at first as CIA Russian "assets" were murdered one by one in the 1980s—ten in all, with a number more imprisoned. Some of the intelligence that had been passed by these assets had kept the United States safe during the Cold War, and their loss made it scarily apparent that the CIA was infected with a mole passing U.S. secrets to foreign intelligence. Grimes, along with her close colleague Jeanne Vertefeuille, never stopped trying to figure out which one of their peers was the traitor. After many years, it was Grimes who connected the suspiciously large bank deposits of colleague Aldrich Ames with meetings he'd had with a Soviet contact. If not for Grimes's discipline, loyalty to her country, and dogged persistence, many more lives may have been lost, and relationships between two superpowers might be very different today.

So, if you want to find behaviors worth emulating and ideals worth following that qualify as Mt. Rushmore grit, look past the depressing headlines and celebrity pap, and I guarantee you'll find authentic grit making news right now, inspiring us not to give up and giving us positive causes to support.

Mt. Olympus grit

Another type of authentic grit includes athletic figures who have risen to extraordinary heights, and in so doing, raised the standards for others to play bigger, outside their physical comfort zone, and to push their bodies and minds to a level that is truly awesome. While some of them are well known, many are not—but all have overcome various setbacks and challenges on the way to either making history in their sport or exhibiting a courage and class that made simply showing up to compete a gritty triumph.

Casey Martin, as mentioned earlier, fits this designation, as do tennis player Serena Williams, swimmer Michael Phelps (post-alcoholism rehab), and Sir Edmund Hillary and Tenzing Norgay, the first people to reach the summit of Mount Everest. Some lesser-knowns with this type of grit have impacted their sport quietly and courageously, like Afghani runner Tahmina Kohistani, who refused to stop training in her war-torn country in spite of widespread denigration and heckling for being a "bad Muslim woman" who ought to "get behind the men." Without much support, training facilities, and other helpful resources, she made the cut for the 2012 London Olympics and ran a best time there, finishing thirty-first out of thirty-two runners. When interviewed after her race, she tearfully shared her story with reporters, noting that although she hadn't won a medal, she was proud of the journey she'd taken, saying, "Being here is more important than a gold medal." And in 2016, the Olympics featured for the first time a squad of refugee athletes who had fled war-torn countries like Syria and who had persevered in their training in spite of indescribable hardship. Their passion and fortitude represent Mt. Olympus grit at its very best.

Time and time again, people with authentic grit demonstrate that winning a trophy or medal isn't what motivates them. What lights them up and gives them a purpose worth waking up for is seeing how far they can go as they attempt to redefine their own limits, or those of their sport, in the case of this type of grit. In so doing, they often provoke others to ponder how they, too, can be more resilient, brave, and gutsy, inspiring them to go out and test their mental and physical mettle in new ways that often change their lives for the better.

Celebrity grit

In 2008, at Harvard University's commencement, J.K. Rowling gave a powerful speech about failure, friendship, and risk-taking, which went viral almost immediately because of its message of how refusing to give up on a dream—in this case, writing about a magical boy named Harry Potter—changed her life, and the lives of millions of others. Like so many parents, I watched all three of my children devour every single Harry Potter book in epic, solitary sessions that they repeated over and over. My daughter even carried the whole series with her to college, turning to them during periods of stress for comfort and familiarity.

How many other mothers like me are grateful to J.K. Rowling for persisting in lonely writing sessions despite being a broke, young, divorced mother? How many of us can thank Rowling for making our kids fall in love with reading? How many sad youngsters found solace in her fantastical world of Hogwarts, a world that kept them from focusing on whatever was troubling them? And how many new authors have been inspired by Rowling's personal story of resilience, starting in humble circumstances but refusing to quit on her dream?

Another common denominator of authentic grit is that the people who possess it never diminish the people they touch; they almost universally cause them instead to become happier or better in some way. Rowling's books are just a small example of what celebrity grit can unleash. Her persistence in writing, along with the values espoused in the Harry Potter books, has been credited with "saving reading" and raising money for enslaved populations around the world.[1]

J.K. Rowling, Oprah Winfrey, Dick Van Dyke, and Spanx founder Sara Blakely all qualify for my celebrity grit designation because they are in the public eye making a difference in the lives of others, and not because they set out to do so, but because their personal stories exemplify authentic grit. Dick Van Dyke, for example, who enjoyed a successful career on the stage and screen, went public with his alcoholism battle in the 1970s, noting that he had always thought he'd be a minister but had found another way to bring hope to others. It's said that with celebrity status comes the burden of being a role model; when a celebrity's actions are rich with authentic grit, we are all doubly blessed.

Ordinary grit

Finally, we take a look at the largest group of people with authentic grit: the unsung heroes who wake up every day and strive to succeed at goals that require persistence and dedication, but that also lack obvious external rewards or attention and acclaim from others. These men and women selflessly take care of disabled children while holding down full-time jobs, tirelessly advocate for the less fortunate as public defenders and social workers despite low pay and depressing outcomes, or learn how to read in their sixties so that they can earn a long-desired high school degree. Although I call it ordinary grit, it is anything but ordinary when you look at what these people do and how they impact their families, communities, and the organizations they are part of.

James Robertson is one such man. For eleven years, he walked twenty-one miles round-trip to his job outside Detroit, where he had a perfect attendance record. In a world filled with many in a new generation who are known to refuse long shifts, early start times, or weekend work, Robertson's daily trudge, due to his insufficient means to buy a car and the lack of adequate public transportation, came to the public's attention through a newspaper article. Within days of its publication, a GoFundMe page had raised $350,000 and the offer of a free car, as well as an outpouring of admiration from around the world. Camera crews documented his shock and tearful acceptance of the car, when he said, "I wish my parents could see me now."

Stories of ordinary grit go viral because we long to see paragons of goodness in a world where the motto for most news is "If it bleeds, it leads," and the view we're given is that of a narcissistic and angry world. When we have an opportunity to witness heroic behavior paired with hard work, humility, and kindness, we are awed and want to share it with others. Research has found that this type of awe has the impact of releasing bonding chemicals in our bodies that enhance our pro-social behavior. So when we hear about a James Robertson, or a man who devotes his days to fixing broken bicycles for underprivileged children, or a woman who matches retirees with newborns who need to be held while they withdraw from a drug addiction inherited from their mother, it's medicine for the soul—and we can't get enough of it.

Authentic grit is everywhere, if we choose to notice it. It is the grandmother driving your kids' school bus while moonlighting at another job to help raise her grandchildren, the inner-city football coach who volunteers his time because he wants to make sure more kids get an opportunity to develop discipline and self-respect, and the pop singer who slept in cars and ate out of trashcans while trying to break into the music business. It is also the grizzled older man at the Alcoholics Anonymous meeting who has been sober for forty years, but who keeps coming to meetings because he knows that just being there inspires others who are struggling to remain sober, too. And there are always more: the woman playing the violin in the subway so she can share her love of classical music with harried commuters, or the first-generation college freshman who is juggling financial, academic, and emotional pressures to take advantage of opportunities that weren't available to her parents.

What you pay attention to will expand

The more I've studied grit in its best forms, the more I've found it. But amidst the din of grim international news, 24-7 news cycles regurgitating stories of problems, and vulgar behavior passing as acceptable in politics and elsewhere, it's possible to overlook it and thus fail to learn from the examples right in front of us. I believe the old saying "What you pay attention to is what expands," so part of the challenge facing us all is to learn how to spot, appreciate, and share with others the qualities that comprise authentic grit.

I want to help you screen out the unending distractions of life that obstruct your path to cultivating humility, willpower, passion, patience, and the other strengths of authentic grit. I want this book to help you clarify and identify the paths and role models that will help you see new ways to grow, change, and flourish in the most difficult circumstances. Have you even come close to imagining what you are capable of? Do you know how to flourish in every setting so that you can live with inspiration and passion, and without regret?

Row your seat

Any type of change in a family, a community, an organization, or the world always starts with one person who shifts their behavior—something that is perfectly captured in the sport of crew in the phrase "Row your seat." If you spend your time criticizing and correcting everyone else who is holding an oar in your boat when the water is choppy and the boat isn't going fast enough, then you are missing your finest opportunity to start an authentic grit movement. So I urge you now to row your own seat in the direction of rugged personal greatness, without expecting anything but the satisfaction of knowing that you are living with passion and a desire to play your best and biggest game in life.

Here are some questions to ponder and write about:

- Name a character from history who epitomizes Mt. Rushmore grit. Describe what they did and the way in which they did it that makes them authentically gritty.

- Do you have a favorite sports figure who may or may not be famous, but who has Mt. Olympus grit? What are some of the characteristics of this person that stand out to you?

- Is there someone in the celebrity world who represents authentic grit to you, who is positive and uplifting? Write down some details about this person, as well as any of their actions that inspire you to stretch your limits and set more difficult goals.

- Name someone with ordinary grit in your life, someone who embodies the qualities of humility, passion, persistence, and hopefulness. Write about how you know this person and what it's like to be around them. In what way does their presence cause you to think or act differently?

Before we get to the information and exercises that will help you develop more good grit, let's take a look at what can happen when grit runs amok, and what you need to know and do in order to avoid going down the tracks that can turn your persistence and passion into fool's gold.

Bad Grit

Faux, Stubborn, and Selfie

handsome, smart, and ambitious, Brian Williams made climbing the network ladder to become the *NBC Nightly News* anchor look easy. With rarely a hair out of place and looking preternaturally young, he reported from war zones, the aftermath of Hurricane Katrina, and other dangerous places at his personal peril, he told viewers. And in speeches before large audiences, he would gravely share how he'd narrowly missed danger, been shot at in helicopters, and watched dead bodies float down streets, all of which he endured because it qualified him to sit in an esteemed television-anchor chair, to report the news honestly and without bias.

But Williams's stories began to publicly unravel in 2015 when a combat veteran wrote in the newspaper *Stars and Stripes* that Williams had made up large parts of his narratives of derring-do, cheapening the bravery of the soldiers who had actually come under fire. It wasn't long before a rush of other stories came out, magnifying many years of embellished yarns, all of which had been designed to make Williams look tougher, braver, and grittier than he really was.

In order to explain why it is important to cultivate the habits and mind-set of authentic grit, it's equally important to look at people who have seeds of the right kind of grit but who fall short of turning their actions into outcomes that make the world better or that inspire others to strive for worthy goals. Brian Williams and the other men and women profiled in this chapter aren't necessarily "bad" people. However, they do provide cautionary tales about how seeking the trappings of fame, money, adulation, and success using some of the strengths that comprise grit, but without evincing key traits like honesty, kindness, and humility, can lead to a flawed outcome. You might find yourself nodding or chuckling as you look through the following examples, but pay attention because they all illustrate how "the little engine" can go off the rails if you don't heed the red flags of narcissism, envy, arrogance, and ignorance that flap wildly in the wind when we go down the wrong track for the wrong reasons.

Faux grit

Brian Williams is a perfect example of "faux grit," which is a quality seen among those who pretend to themselves or others that they have achieved difficult things, but who have taken shortcuts or faked those accomplishments to obtain admiration. Although many people readily admit to puffing themselves up at times to impress a romantic interest or a potential employer, faux grit takes this quality to a whole different level because of what the people allege to have accomplished. Specifically, these people choose outcomes that put them into a select, sometimes elite, group, despite knowing that they have not done, and probably cannot do, the hard work that's commensurate with those goals.

Many people think that falsely appropriating the mantle of war hero is one of the most repugnant lies a person can tell because military service is almost universally admired, irrespective of country or background. Some of the most egregious examples I found of faux grit are men claiming to be recipients of the Medal of Honor, the highest award given in the U.S. armed services. The award is so coveted and so rare that there are currently only seventy-nine living Medal of Honor awardees, all decorated for "gallantry and intrepidity at the risk of his life above and beyond the call of duty while engaged in an action against an enemy of the United States."[1]

Appallingly, many men have been caught purchasing fake Medal of Honor medals online and at flea markets, even going so far as to put the false award on their résumés and riding in parades that honor combat veterans and other heroes. Paul Bucha, president of the Congressional Medal of Honor Society, believes that part of the reason people claim high honors they haven't earned is because our society prizes "winners," and some believe that their normal lives and actions just aren't sufficient to feel good about themselves. Faux grit, he speculates, is a natural outgrowth of feeling the pressure to achieve important goals in order to feel validated. And if you believe you don't have what it takes to be a winner and that you are not worthy enough without that title, it may seem better to misappropriate honors you haven't earned than to figure out what else you could offer the world to give your life purpose.

"Why do we use connections to get into a college we normally couldn't get into?" Bucha asks. "Why do we use human growth hormones in the Olympics? For that matter, why do we send NBA basketball players to the Olympics? Second place is not good enough. We've placed such tremendous value on cosmetics. Winning has become everything. That's the society in which a faker or a fraud presents himself."[2]

Politicians who are looking for popularity and votes aren't above faux grit. Several examples of those who have embellished their war service include Ronald Reagan, who was grounded stateside during his military career because of poor eyesight but who made his time sound more dangerous than it was. Former Veterans Affairs Secretary Robert McDonald falsely boasted about being in the Special Forces, and Mark Kirk, congressman turned senator, incorrectly stated that he'd earned a coveted naval commendation. Hillary Clinton was also criticized for saying that she'd run across the tarmac while dodging bullets in Bosnia in 1992, when video footage of the trip shows her waving, smiling, and shaking hands upon her arrival.

Real estate developer and President Donald Trump, not surprisingly, has his own brand of faux grit. Although he's known for his braggadocio, boasting about his success in virtually all departments of life (which qualifies for yet another kind of negative grit), he doesn't actually pretend that he served in the military. He goes one step further, stating that his time at the New York Military Academy "always felt like [I] was in the military" because he received "more training militarily than a lot of the guys that go into the military."[3]

When winning at all costs is the coveted prize, it's inevitable that someone will take shortcuts—like the pervasive "redshirting" in sports and even academics—which is often when faux grit pops up in the sporting world. Use of banned substances, such as anabolic steroids and human growth hormone, to achieve athletic domination has tainted many of the world championships and Olympics in recent years. In a sign of collective disdain for what superstar baseball players like Barry Bonds and Roger Clemens, products of "the Steroids Era," did to get ahead, voters are casting fewer and fewer votes for them in the annual Hall of Fame balloting. This shift seems to indicate that the stated qualifications of "integrity, sportsmanship, and character" are being honored more than faux grit when it comes to picking our baseball heroes.[4]

Reaching elite swimming levels usually involves many years of brutal twice-a-day practice, weight lifting, 4 a.m. wake-ups, and untold personal sacrifices. Some swimmers can go years without improving their times, even while maintaining this exhausting regimen. That's why Irish swimmer Michelle Smith raised so many eyebrows when she won three gold medals at the 1996 Olympics. Suspicions were raised by her inexplicable time drops at the age of twenty-six, after never reaching the top levels of the sport, and also because she got involved with a Dutch cyclist who'd been banned from his sport for doping. Smith was caught tampering with a urine sample by spiking it with alcohol when she was randomly drug tested a year after the Olympics, and was banned from the sport for four years. Her subsequent retirement ended her career, but the suspension left a bad taste in the mouths of her Olympic competitors because being caught out of season meant that she has been allowed to keep her medals.[5]

Perhaps the most egregious case of faux grit in recent sporting history is that of Lance Armstrong, the cyclist who built an industry and persona around being the survivor of testicular cancer and who then, allegedly without any unnatural aids, created a superhuman body and honed his will of iron to ride to multiple Tour de France victories. His nonprofit foundation, Livestrong, basked in the aura of being headed by a man so gritty that even cancer couldn't stop him. Armstrong continued to rake in millions of dollars in prize money, endorsements, and appearance fees as he perpetuated his fraud on the world for over ten years.

Former teammates blew the whistle on Armstrong after being summoned to testify under oath about what they'd witnessed and participated in. Armstrong responded with viciousness, threatening harm and suing his accusers, ruining their livelihoods and reputations in several instances. For several more years, he managed to dupe the public with his faux grit story while privately paying doctors and suppliers for the substances that would allow him to ride hard, recover quickly, and win. Eventually, the whole house of cards fell. Now Armstrong lives in semi-isolation and ignominy, banned for life from the sport that he rode to glory and reviled by his former teammates, who were crushed in his quest to achieve victory and be seen as an indomitable champion.[6]

Our society is filled with faux grit in universities and other professional settings, too. Numerous scandals have erupted in medical and psychology departments at elite universities, where researchers have been caught falsifying data, often because of an unwillingness to put in the unglamorous years of sifting through results to find statistical significance and noteworthy findings.[7] Getting a doctorate or tenure by plagiarizing is another faux grit shortcut that has soared in recent years. After all, why put in seven or more years researching and writing something original when it's so much easier to pretend someone else's work is yours? And what about those who put in for overtime at jobs by falsifying timecards, claiming to be the hardest-working people in the office?

This behavior often takes criminal turns, as it did in the fall of 2010, when grandmother Lela West, a respected and powerful volunteer in the sport of rowing—who even sat on the national board that selects Olympic rowers—was found to have embezzled half a million dollars over ten years from the Virginia Scholastic Rowing Association. Throughout her stealing career, she had been dubbed the "queen of rowing" because of her generous donation of hundreds of unpaid hours to the organization. "I don't have time for a paying job," she insisted to one newspaper with false humility.[8]

We see faux grit in corporations as well, where shortcuts have been taken to attain easy wins, and greed is often at the root of the motivation for this immoral behavior; the scandals at Enron and Wells Fargo are just two recent examples. One of the most cleverly titled articles in the history of *Harvard Business Review*, "Goals Gone Wild," details the corporate disasters that have occurred when a lofty goal is set and corners are cut to get to the finish line to receive money, acclaim, or both.[9] For example, Ford Motor Company's desire to break new ground in the auto world by creating a 2,000-pound car for $2,000, in six months, resulted in a defective and dangerous automobile that burst into flames in rear-end collisions—something they knew they could have avoided with reinforced bumpers. Ford Motor's decision, led by the brash and arrogant Lee Iacocca, ended up killing or maiming nine hundred people.[10]

Faux grit is distinct from authentic grit in many ways, most notably because people with authentic grit have humility and are the last to brag about themselves. The person with faux grit wants you to know how much they've done, how hard they've worked, and how tough they are, and they revel in the trappings of their alleged success, whether it's giving interviews about their accomplishments, tweeting pictures of framed yellow jerseys from the Tour de France (which Lance Armstrong did), or waving in a Fourth of July parade while wearing fake medals bought at a flea market. Instead of naturally attracting others because of an authentic aura, people with faux grit eventually repel others by over-promoting themselves, which then causes them to lose all sympathy with others when their misdeeds are discovered.

Stubborn grit

On May 19, 2012, Shriya Shah-Klorfine reached the summit of Mount Everest. After years of dreaming about reaching the peak of the world's highest mountain, this Canadian woman did it, reveling in the experience for an hour and taking pictures. As her husband noted later, "If she wanted something, there was nothing you could say to stop her." He added, "She was very strong-willed—you could say Type A." But after Shah-Klorfine started her descent from Everest's summit, it was already too late. She'd shrugged off warnings from others in her party that she should have turned around much earlier in the day, not just because she was upping her own chances of dying but also because her actions were putting others at risk. As feared, the Canadian dreamer eventually stopped walking—or moving at all. Sherpas dragged her along for hours, but she died nonetheless. Her body was brought down ten days later.[11]

Grit, right? Passion and perseverance in pursuit of a long-term goal? Yes. But authentic grit? Absolutely not. Shriya Shah-Klorfine exhibited something I call "stubborn grit," which I define as "the obstinate pursuit of a long-term goal that presents more negatives than positives because circumstances have changed."

Although Shah-Klorfine had long dreamt of summiting Mount Everest, she didn't actually know much about climbing, nor did she have the requisite training that qualified people know is essential to make this brutal climb, which often involves years of intensive technical training, plus mental and physical preparation. What she had, instead, was tenacity and money. Instead of putting in the years of unassuming, hard work that defines authentic grit, she paid a Nepalese company, Utmost Adventure Trekking, which had never actually guided anyone to the top, to get her there. They agreed, promising to teach her everything she needed to know, which even included how to put on crampons, or ice-climbing foot spikes, for her boots.

The Sherpas, Nepalese who accompany most parties because of their generations of experience and unique physical capacities, expressed concern about Shah-Klorfine's inadequacies from the get-go, but to no avail. She was slower than everyone else and arrogant about what she thought she could overcome simply because she was fit and didn't experience altitude headaches. "I talked with her, and every time she said, 'I can do it. I can do it. I can do it,'" Utmost's company manager, Rishi Raj Kadel, said later, defending the decision to let her climb.

When climbers are drunk on their vision of summitting a mountain, having invested their time, money, and ego in reaching the peak of a vaunted site like Mount Everest, they are vulnerable to something that mountaineers call "summit fever." Summit fever is the irrational state of pushing to the top of a mountain in spite of gathering storm clouds or ominous weather conditions that foretell an imminent whiteout or blizzard. Summit fever erases good judgment, putting your own and possibly others' lives at risk because you are desperate to claim the prize and earn bragging rights to say you got to the top.[12]

The same type of maniacal drive and poor decision-making can be seen underwater when a scuba diver attempts a dive that is beyond their skill level or training, sometimes to obtain bragging rights, like snagging a piece of china from the sunken ocean liner the *Andrea Doria*. One of the most tragic stories of deep-water stubborn grit is detailed in the book *The Last Dive,* in which the father-son duo, Chris and Chrissy Rouse, brazenly pursued fame and flouted good judgment in their quest to solve the mystery of a sunken German U-boat off the coast of New Jersey. They both died an agonizing death from "the bends" on their last dive together, which was also partly the result of "the rapture of the deep," the same false sense of well-being that climbers feel with summit fever, when thin air makes clear thinking difficult.[13]

Whether you call it summit fever, rapture of the deep, or stubborn grit, they are all indicative of a persistence to pursue an ambitious goal long after it no longer makes sense. Stubborn grit is the entrepreneur who doesn't heed the signs that their product is no longer viable and who throws good money after bad, working long hours to try to prove their point, ignoring the pleas and advice of people who try to help them see the situation more clearly and pull up stakes before it is too late. Stubborn grit is the athlete who plays through injury and exhaustion to their detriment, like the thirteen University of Iowa football players who found themselves hospitalized with rhabdomyolysis in January 2013 after exceeding their bodies' capabilities in exhausting workouts, which resulted in muscle breakdown that infected their kidneys.[14] Stubborn grit is also the dieter who doesn't know when to stop losing weight and crosses into the dangerous territory of anorexia nervosa. (Sufferers of this eating disorder are similar to some mountain climbers and scuba divers who don't know when to stop. Anorexics' brains don't work effectively when they drop below critical body weight, and if they don't listen to the advice of medical professionals or well-meaning friends who truly care, they risk losing their lives.)

Stubborn grit is especially sad when an elite athlete ignores warning symptoms that their body has been pushing too hard for too long, eventually costing them their career. This is exactly what befell one of America's top marathoners, whose meteoric running career came to an untimely end in 2015. Ryan Hall punished his body for years, routinely running at least a hundred miles each week and using unconventional training methods prior to the 2012 London Olympics, including training at marathon pace, running 4:42 miles for long stretches. He now says that although he thrived at elite levels for years—winning the national championship in the 5000 meters while at Stanford, and later running the fastest marathon time ever by an American man (2:04)—overtraining backfired on him just as he was about to reach his potential. Hall's testosterone levels are now so chronically low, and he is so fatigued, that he made the difficult decision to leave the sport when the best minds in medicine couldn't help him. As he ruefully reflects on his years of running, he notes that he wasn't sure if he'd ever "let [his] body come to baseline. I don't even know what baseline is."[15]

A telltale sign of stubborn grit is hubris. Unlike the narcissism and entitlement seen in faux grit, stubborn grit's hubris is embodied by the person who believes that they have the superhuman ability to pull rabbits out of hats—be those hats physical, emotional, or financial—and does the hard work necessary to succeed, but doesn't heed the signs that it no longer makes sense to stay the course. Serena Williams, one of the best women's tennis players in history, has pleaded guilty to stubborn grit at times, noting, "I have a stopping issue. I don't have a quit button. You just can't press control-alt-delete with me." Her solution? She told her family and support system: "Listen, if I'm sick, just beat me if you have to, hold me down, like don't let me go out."[16]

Unlike authentic grit, stubborn grit doesn't inspire others; instead, it makes one wonder why those who have it can't see reality. Stubborn grit is the contestant on *American Idol* who sings off-key, but is shocked when the judges tell them that they don't have talent, and then flounces off stage, insisting that they're going to prove everyone wrong by continuing to pursue singing as a career because "everyone" has always told them how talented they are. Think participation trophies and inflated praise for many Millennials, which has eliminated honesty from many conversations about talent in recent decades.

Part of the reason people have trouble stepping away from goals that no longer make sense can be explained by the economic theory of sunk costs. Research shows that once we have invested a lot of time and energy into an activity—marriage or building a career, for example—we don't want to "book a loss" and walk away. This is a natural human tendency, epitomized by the saying "Losing hurts worse than winning feels good."[17] But part of having authentic grit is building self-awareness, as well as a savvy team of supporters and advisors who will help you know when to quit and stop investing time, money, and energy into something that no longer makes sense. The hubris of stubborn grit causes you to make decisions alone or in an echo chamber of yes-men, who never challenge a person's ego or authority. Ed Deci, cofounder of self-determination theory, has found that decisions made alone are never the best decisions, which is why having the right posse of friends, advisers, and colleagues is so critical.[18]

Selfie grit

Robert O'Neill burst into the media glare in the fall of 2014 when he broke the code of "the quiet professionals" who make up the United States Special Forces units. In spite of taking an oath to keep all mission details confidential, O'Neill identified himself as the Navy SEAL who had killed Osama bin Laden in the raid on his Pakistani compound in 2011. "I shot him, two times in the forehead," O'Neill said to *Esquire* magazine. "Bap! Bap! The second time, as he is going down. He crumpled to the floor in front of his bed and I hit him again."[19]

O'Neill's decision to take credit and share details of the confidential raid infuriated his former colleagues and drew the contempt of others in the Special Forces fraternity, who unanimously said that he'd violated the ethos of the brotherhood. Perhaps reflective of his generation's desire to be famous and admired, O'Neill's ego went against one of the oft-cited sayings in the military: "There is no 'I' in team." In late 2015, ISIS published O'Neill's home address on social media, naming him their number-one assassination target.[20]

Selfie grit is a variant of faux grit and stubborn grit in several important ways. The person with selfie grit brags about their achievements but *did* actually accomplish them, unlike the person with faux grit. Nor have they failed and overshot the mark with their goals, as do many who exhibit stubborn grit. Selfie grit is unique; I define it as "the relentless glorification of one's pursuit of difficult goals, including triumph over challenging obstacles, real or imagined." The reason I include the disclaimer "imagined" is that, on occasion, a person has accomplished a challenging goal, but they haven't quite walked the difficult path they want you to believe they did. Selfie grit reeks of narcissism.

Another example of a person with selfie grit is football player Johnny Manziel, the electric quarterback at Texas A&M University who won the Heisman Trophy as a freshman. As he became more celebrated and broke more records, his behavior became ruder and more aggressive. He taunted opposing teams and the public, often rubbing his fingers together in the "money" symbol to indicate his triumphs, and he was never shy about self-promotion with his social-media selfies.[21] Manziel was drafted twenty-second in the 2014 NFL football draft by the Cleveland Browns, but it wasn't long before he was in even more trouble, this time with alcohol and domestic violence charges. By the end of the 2015 season, he had all but thrown away his chances of NFL glory, with his team cutting him and even both of his agents resigning. A little bit more humility and self-regulation—two components of authentic grit—might have saved Manziel and allowed his talent to find a home with a professional team. Not unsurprisingly, he also exhibits stubborn grit, because instead of listening to his family and friends who fear for his life, at this book's writing he continues to drink and use drugs, insisting that he doesn't have a problem.

Who is self-made?

One of the things that really stood out to me in my interviews with people who have authentic grit was how often they were quick to point out the support they'd gotten from others in their goal pursuits. The opposite is always true when you scrutinize the stories of people with selfie grit; they use the pronouns "I" and "me" more than any other term and almost never thank anyone else for being part of their success.

Football is one of the most popular sports in the United States, which is how stardom and fame can come so easily to a college phenom like Johnny Manziel. Showboating isn't uncommon, but some teams discourage it or levy penalties for excessive celebration. The University of Notre Dame has always removed the names from the back of the football jerseys to drive home the message that no one is more special than anyone else. In one scene in the Showtime documentary *A Season With,* which covered Notre Dame through the 2015 football season, a coach is seen admonishing a player for grandstanding after he had an especially good play: "You think you did that all yourself?" he demands. "What about the linemen and the other players who made it possible for you to do what you did? Don't ever act that way again!"[22]

Bad bunker grit

Circling back to my question in Chapter 4 about whether or not Adolph Hitler, the mastermind of the evil extermination program of the Holocaust, had grit—it's obvious that he had grit, but it was the worst kind. He was notoriously self-absorbed, narcissistic, and intolerant of opposing viewpoints, so he surrounded himself with people who told him what he wanted to hear, reinforcing his worldview, even while his nation was crumbling around him.

To build authentic grit, we can't hide in a bunker of our own making. Today it's very easy to shut out ideas we don't like. On-demand services and apps can easily let us create an echo chamber where we get our own custom-tailored news and filter out anyone who doesn't preach to our personal choir. That sort of insulation can turn our passion into a self-feeding obsession, and the case of Hitler provides a stark reminder of how dangerous such behavior can be. When we have authentic grit, we cultivate flexibility. We accept that we will be challenged to analyze, question, and often adapt our ideas and our approach to life.

So now that we have looked at all aspects of grit, both good and bad, let's take a look at how I propose we build authentic grit.

part 2

7

Baking the Grit Cake

there are a number of qualities that stand out in people with authentic grit: humility, determination, persistence, self-control, and optimism, to name a few. But as I pondered how to create a motivational guide to getting gritty, I realized that my recipe needed to come with a warning. Much like a cake that tastes different when you leave out one ingredient, cook it too long, bake it at the wrong altitude or in the wrong pan, or forget to mix the ingredients thoroughly, it's not enough just to follow the instructions in this book, one chapter at a time, and hope for the best. Developing authentic grit means experimenting with these ideas, practicing them over and over, learning what works through trial and error, and evolving from a cook who masters one behavior at a time to a master chef who blends them all together repeatedly with hard work and for the right reasons.

If you demonstrate self-control one day, but not regularly, or you can persist when you want to, but not most of the time, then you will not cultivate authentic grit—instead, you are someone who is dabbling in grit. If you develop a purpose, but don't set goals and get feedback about fulfilling your destiny, you are just another dreamer. And if you choose to give to others only when it suits you, instead of building a team of reciprocal relationships powered by generosity and altruism, you may achieve some of your goals, but you will always celebrate alone.

My martial-arts sensei, Paul Thomas, likes to quiz his students to make a similar point about what they are doing and why. He will stop class, perform isolated punches, kicks, takedowns, and forms with precise beauty, and ask, "Am I a martial artist when I do this?" If they nod, they are wrong.

"That is someone doing the martial arts," he will sternly correct them. "A martial artist is someone who has the knowledge, the abilities, and the mind-set to know how to attack, when to attack, and what to do in a variety of circumstances. A martial artist is someone who is humble enough to learn from lower belts and to respect all opponents. A martial artist is someone who meets your eyes and doesn't run from challenge. A martial artist is someone who can blend the moves together into graceful harmony. The person who just comes to class and does kicks and punches is not a martial artist yet. That is someone who does the martial arts."

Just as becoming a martial artist takes time, developing authentic grit will take time and, at times, tax your patience. I like to caution clients that everything we work on together—purpose, intrinsic goals, willpower, positive relationships, environmental cues, and more—is interdependent, and that leaving out any one element when they are pursuing hard goals will be like baking a cake and leaving out a key ingredient. For example, if you work on upping your emotional flourishing but are surrounded by naysayers, you can undo your progress as quickly as you build it. If your humility and patience come and go, depending on how you feel from day to day, how can you expect great results? And if you can't delay gratification, why work on setting and pursuing difficult goals at all?

Now that you have a good idea about how grit can be both well used and misused, I want you to read the following chapters and think about what you need to do to improve your own grittiness in a variety of untested ways. Don't try to change everything at once. Start with a chapter that pertains to something you want to work on, and follow the suggestions at the end of the chapter to see what works best for you in getting the results you want. You might even want to engage in this process with likeminded individuals, possibly in a mastermind group or a work team. The exercises are designed to be fun as well as thoughtful. Some are writing exercises, while others ask you to think about a new behavior, go out and practice it, and then come back to report on the results. Many of the exercises can be used over and over, so copy them so that you have extras for yourself, family, friends, coworkers, and anyone else you'd like to share your gritty journey with. Track progress and celebrate it. "Gamify" the process, if you will. Why not enjoy yourself along the way to a grittier you?

The gold medal of authentic grit and where it leads

In the weeks leading up to the 2016 Rio Olympics, I was watching an interview on television with the victorious 1996 women's Olympic gymnastics team when I heard Kerri Strug say something important about how the display of grit changes you forever. Let me first set the stage.

In 1996, the U.S. women entered the Olympic games with the goal of winning the team title, something that had been the sole province of the Russian women since 1948. To prepare, they isolated themselves in an Emory University fraternity house, surrounded by police tape and chains, so that they could bond, focus on their goal, and visualize success. Then, as they competed in the final round of the routines, the U.S. team had a slim lead when one of their stars, Dominique Moceanu, fell twice on the vault—which was unheard of. Maintaining their slight edge to keep the win came down to Kerri Strug, the quiet, less decorated teen, who also wasn't the team's best vaulter.

Determined to be the person who sealed the win for the United States, Strug squared herself off and ran down the runway and did the difficult vault, but after she landed, she fell to the mat in searing pain as two ligaments tore in her left ankle. Her fall indicated to Bela Karolyi, the team's coach, that Strug would have to vault again in spite of her obvious agony: "Kerri, we need you one more time for the gold," he said. As Strug remembers, she got to her feet and said, "This is the Olympics. I can do this," and then she said a prayer and lined up to go again.

Somehow, in spite of the throbbing in her ankle, Strug ran seventy-five feet like a woman possessed, vaulted and spun through the air, and then landed perfectly. Quickly lifting the injured foot, she hopped from one side to the other to smile at the judges, and then she fell to her knees. The auditorium went wild, and people leapt to their feet screaming as the Russians watched helplessly. Strug's vaults saved the day, and when she went up with her teammates to accept the gold medals, she had to be carried by Karolyi and placed gently beside her fellow gymnasts, her foot heavily bandaged.

Strug had practiced her routines and vaults thousands of times leading up to the Olympic Games, and in the moment that she most needed to perform, she pulled everything together to succeed. Carrying out everything separately—doing the training, having humility, demonstrating perseverance, building the mind-set of toughness, and leaning on her spiritual faith—was not nearly as powerful as when she had to weave it all together when it counted the most. This was not someone doing gymnastics; this was an Olympic gymnast who had grit when the situation called for the utmost in guts, focus, and calm under pressure.

The results of what Strug did that day went far beyond winning the gold medal and giving the United States a much-desired win. It did exactly what authentic grit does for anyone who has the willingness to build it and use it: it changed her as a human being and opened her up to tackling other things in subsequent years. "That vault signifies a lot more than people understand," Strug says now. "Because when all eyes were on me, I dealt with the pressure, and now, how I view myself and what I'm capable of is very different because of that vault."

Now you can prepare for your own Olympic vault

The following chapters are written in the order I felt was most logical, given what I've seen in so many clients over the years. But since everyone is different, I invite you to find the right place for you to start this work. Like Kerri Strug, you may have to do a lot of tedious work over the years to develop the toughness and resilience you desire. Know that it will pay off with lots of little wins, which will give you confidence and happiness, and build the stage for you to be ready when that Olympic moment comes for some of your biggest goals. You may not feel ready when it happens, but trust your training, put your brain into the right gear, and then make a run for it. You'll probably stick the landing, and your life will never be the same again.

8

Building Passion to Fuel Purpose

n 2003, Jack Hairston was a depressed retired guy in south Florida, with no passion and no obvious reason for being alive. That all changed the day a young man's bike broke down in front of his house. Since he was good with a wrench, Hairston went outside and helped the young man get back on his bike with a few tweaks, which ended up being the difference between the young man's getting to work that day to earn money and not getting there at all.

Soon word spread that Hairston could fix bikes, and people starting showing up with them at his front door. Instead of feeling useless and depressed, Hairston found himself looking forward to each day because he suddenly felt like he had a purpose. With his wrench and know-how, he could make a difference in others' lives, which he said made his own life feel like it was worth living again.

Sixteen years later, Hairston has gone from fixing up a few bikes to overseeing a warehouse for repaired bicycles, as well as one of the biggest bicycle giveaways in the country at Christmas. His charity, Jack the Bike Man, is staffed by an army of volunteers, who give their time to fix bikes for a small fee as well as provide opportunities for underprivileged children to learn how to work with bikes, help others, and always have a way to get around.

Hairston feels that being on a bicycle improves the community, connects people, gives them hope, and allows families to have access to transportation that they wouldn't otherwise have. His Christmas giveaway, one of the most anticipated days for many families in the region, lights up the lives of hundreds of children who otherwise would have no presents. What started as a small inconvenience ended up saving Hairston's life, giving it newfound passion and purpose.

Burning goals

To have grit, you have to have passion. Without passion, it's too difficult to persist when times are hard and solutions are elusive. Without passion, it's too difficult to remind yourself of the importance of your journey when others doubt or criticize you. Without passion, you won't be able to screen out the noisy disturbances that undo less committed individuals. Without passion, it's too hard to connect with others about the importance of your mission and convince them to help you and get on board. Without passion, it's just another workmanlike goal, and not necessarily the mission that will change your life—or the world. But how do you get passion? And how does it connect with purpose?

Walter Mischel, the researcher behind the "Marshmallow Test," which discovered the long-term benefits of delaying gratification, says that when we have a "burning goal" or a passion that lights us up, it's easier to marshal the inner resources to work hard, say no to temptation, and see projects through to the finish line. When Mischel was eight years old, the Germans annexed Austria, and he and his family of Jewish intellectuals fled to the United States, never quite regaining their economic status. But Mischel's grandmother would lecture him on the importance of *sitzfleisch* (summoning up the inner resources to continue to work hard in spite of obstacles), and Mischel did just that with his newfound passion of making "a life that would help my family recover from the trauma of suddenly becoming homeless refugees," which later morphed into a passion for helping children learn how to cope with trauma.[1]

Mischel is typical of the person who discovers their passion by experiencing a setback and then decides to do something to make sure that others don't go through the same experience, or that they have better coping tools if they do. That's what happened to me with my eating disorder: when I successfully overcame it, I realized I had a passion for bringing enthusiasm to each day—a deep, internal recognition of the fact that we are privileged to be alive, regardless of how hopeless life might seem at times. My purpose flowed from that passion. Through coaching, speaking, writing, and educating, I try to bring hope and tools of positive change to help other people live their best lives right now, as well as to accomplish the difficult goals that will make the biggest difference in their lives.

So finding one's passion might come by surprise and could be the result of experiencing trauma. Amy Gleicher is another example of someone who found her passion for a cause by surviving difficult circumstances. In 1988, after marrying a widower, Warren, who'd lost his wife in a car accident, and adopting his two sons, Jon and Adam, she gave birth to a son, Max, with fragile X syndrome, a genetic condition that causes intellectual disability, and behavioral and learning challenges. "I asked the doctor if he would ever go to college or get married, and he said, 'No,'" she remembers now, looking back. By the time Max turned five, Amy's life was a blur of exhaustion, isolation, and a crash course in motherhood that would wear down most people and sap their passion for life. But instead of falling apart, Amy channeled her energy into developing a grittier approach to life so that Max and his brothers could all live their best lives.

She adapted to the demands of helping Jon and Adam learn how to create lives of stability and normalcy after the devastating loss of their mother, and she reluctantly faced the fact that she and Warren wouldn't be able to provide Max with the twenty-four-hour-a-day environment of trained support that his condition required. After years of researching and tirelessly advocating for Max, she got him a hard-won, coveted spot at Heartbeet, a community in Vermont that houses men and women like Max in a farm environment, where they can have their own lives of purpose surrounded by people who can give them the care they deserve. Amy says that she is grateful for the lessons Max brought her and believes that becoming a mother gave her the passion and grit that have made life rich and meaningful. "Everyone deserves a warrior," she says. "These children turned me into a warrior, and I'm a better person because of it."

Obsessive passion vs. harmonious passion

Bob Vallerand is the perfect person to be the world's expert on the topic of passion. When you meet him, he exudes high energy, makes direct eye contact, and leans forward while speaking effusively about his findings on what he calls "harmonious" and "obsessive" passions. A former basketball player with aspirations to play at an elite level, Vallerand loves to talk about the sport to illustrate the differences between having a positive type of passion that makes you happier, wiser, and more willing to contribute to society (harmonious) and having the kind that causes you to ruminate, be sapped of vitality, and neglect other important areas of life (obsessive). A harmonious passion is one that you look forward to and that fills your daydreams in a positive way, while an obsessive passion is marked by intrusive thoughts and difficulty controlling the urge to do the activity. Think about the difference between a mate who is respectful, treats you well, and gives without strings attached versus a mate who is jealous, controlling, and takes more from you than they give.

"Look at Bill Bradley," Vallerand explains. "He is someone who was passionate about basketball and played at a high level in the NBA with the New York Knicks, but he never stopped growing in other areas. He was a Rhodes Scholar and went on to serve as a U.S. senator. He never identified just as a basketball player, and was able to explore other passions like getting a master's in political science at Oxford while also winning the European basketball championship playing for an Italian team. This helped open the door to a second career in politics." Vallerand says that other examples of harmonious passion are people who donate time to causes like Doctors Without Borders, as well as those who are able to come back from difficult experiences with a better perspective on life.

People with obsessive passion, on the other hand, ruminate about what they can't do and are unable to disconnect from their passion. Vallerand points to the number of top sports performers who have obsessive passion, which is why they cannot successfully move on when their careers end. It's also why so many college athletes report pervasive feelings of distress and anxiety during their competitive years. The constant measurement and assessment of talent and competence are more than many of these athletes can handle, particularly when their core self-concept is so closely tied to their performance. They don't have a growth mind-set to give them resilience and help them get through slug-gish or injury-filled periods. After their athletic careers end, some may struggle for years to find something that feels as positive and affirming as what they experienced as athletes, which is why they struggle with self-worth and confidence. Professional organizations like the National Football League are aware of this problem and now encourage players to plan for their post-professional lives—to spend time learning new skills and hobbies—reducing the difficulty of moving on from a life of obsessive passion into one that might be devoid of passion.

Two passions?

Consistent with the findings that harmonious passion adds happiness to life, while obsessive passion detracts from it, new research from the *Journal of Positive Psychology* finds that having two harmonious passions is actually better than having just one. Benjamin Schellenberg and Daniel Bailis asked more than a thousand college undergraduates about their favorite activities, and those who reported having two harmonious passions scored higher in well-being and happiness than those who reported having either one harmonious passion or none at all, indicating that there is an additive benefit to finding joy in two positive activities. Any parent with more than one child will understand why this is so because the arrival of a second or third child never seems to detract from the joy you experience with your first- or second-born; you simply have more love to give to everyone.

Moving from obsessive passion into harmonious passion

Legendary swimmer Michael Phelps is a great example of someone who lived with a miserable, obsessive passion—for swimming and winning—from a young age until well into his twenties. His public tribulations after the 2012 Olympics with depression and recreational drug and alcohol use led to a DUI that sent him into an emotional free fall and landed him in a rehab center. As with so many similar stories, hitting bottom is what caused Phelps to honestly examine his demons as well as his inner motivations for swimming and then to do a reboot that saved his life and refueled his sense of purpose. The obsessive passion that once drove him to suicidal thoughts was transformed into a harmonious passion that allowed him to train with joyful abandon and a primal love for the sport. As a result, he became, at age thirty-one, the first man to qualify for five different Olympic games. He then cemented his athletic legacy and became the most decorated Olympian of all time by adding five golds and one silver to his overall haul in Rio—for a grand total of twenty-eight lifetime Olympic medals, twenty-three of those gold. Phelps's passion for winning evolved into a passion for finding out what new frontiers he could create in a sport he loved, and instead of resenting the daily grind that allowed him to finish his swimming career on a high note, he focused on the joy it brought him and how it inspired so many others to swim—the "Phelps effect," it's now called.

What *isn't* passion

Passion is what you wake up for and look forward to expressing. Having "interests" is a completely different animal. I frequently find that clients of mine who record low grit scores, and who carry regrets about unfulfilled goals, have lots of interests, but nothing that's ever turned into a bona fide passion. They love to explore new ideas and are early adopters, but they don't always have the needed stick-to-it-iveness when it comes to seeing things through to the end. Some of this is because of their attention span, some of it is because they truly thrive on novelty and need to keep moving, and some of it is because it's human nature to be enthusiastic when starting something, but then fail to have the passion to see it through. In fact, a comparison of five thirty-day video-teaching series found that viewership drops by half after the first day of instruction, and that fewer than 10 percent ever get to the last video.[2]

If you think you have interests, but not passions, consider taking one of the stronger interests and doing something deeper with it. Sometimes you need to fully immerse yourself in something to see if it takes root and quickens your pulse. If you are dabbling in an instrument but haven't taken a lesson, take that first lesson and don't quit until you've put in several months of effort. If you are fascinated by a certain type of learning, sign up online for a course and finish it. Just like young children who can't develop a passion for anything until they've mastered the tedious fundamentals—for example, chess, piano, or the multiplication tables—as adults, we have to get past the early-exploration phase to find out if something really lights us up, and making ourselves accountable to others helps us do just that.

There's another reason to try to turn an interest into a hobby, and that's because having too many interests but no consuming passion is like dating a lot of people but never getting married and discovering the passion that comes from a long-term, committed relationship with just one person. When you always keep doors open in your mind and dabble in many things, it actually consumes so much energy that you have nothing left to give fully to any one thing. Psychology researcher Dan Ariely, author of *Predictably Irrational,* says that studies at the Massachusetts Institute of Technology found that people hate to "close doors" on future options, even when it's unlikely those options will ever pan out. But the end result is less time and focus for the things that really matter, so Ariely suggests that people narrow their lives down to the options that matter most and that create the greatest emotional payoff. Marie Kondo, the Japanese decluttering expert, says the same thing and encourages people whose lives are full of "stuff" to let go of anything that doesn't "spark joy."[3] If something doesn't spark joy, then it should be thrown out, donated, and expunged because it brings us down in ways we probably can't even see.

Passion drives purpose

The more you examine lives of authentic grit, the more you see that passion is part and parcel of understanding a person's purpose. Take Wayne Pacelle, a lobbyist in Washington, DC, whose passion has always been for animals. This passion led him to his purpose: to prevent humans from abusing animals. A Yale University graduate, he adopted a vegan lifestyle thirty years ago as a young man and has worked tirelessly to help the plight of animals wherever they are exploited. He played an important role in negotiating with SeaWorld to phase out the breeding of killer whales for shows, in getting stores like PetSmart and Petco to stop selling puppies from puppy mills, in stopping Ringling Bros. and Barnum & Bailey Circus from continuing their elephant acts, and in halting the use of chimpanzees in medical tests at the National Institutes of Health.

Without authentic grit, though, and an unwillingness to give up on some of his biggest goals, Pacelle wouldn't have achieved one of his biggest coups. After years of not making headway in reaching anyone at McDonald's, which buys one in every seven pigs in the United States, Pacelle got a call one day from the billionaire Carl Icahn, asking what he could do to be helpful. Pacelle described the inhumane treatment of pigs at commercial breeding farms, where they are confined for years in crates so small they can't walk or turn around, becoming so agitated that they chew the bars until their teeth crack and bang their snouts and foreheads to a bloody pulp. Icahn swung into action and "effortlessly" reached the CEO of McDonald's and other companies, opening the door for Pacelle to come in and make his case. McDonald's ultimately agreed to give up buying pigs from farms that used crates, which caused sixty other food suppliers like Burger King, Wendy's, and Carl's Jr. to do the same. That laid the groundwork for Walmart, the world's largest food seller, to adopt new guidelines for its suppliers, directing them to adopt humane policies, too.[4]

What if you feel passionless?

Occasionally, people come to me for help because they've simply burned out on life and don't feel like they have any passion for anything. In the process of working, raising children, and dealing with the disappointments of life, they've lost track of what lights them up. In some cases, they got onto a specific track early in life because they felt they had to make a choice about a career, and they chose steadiness over passion.

This was the case with a young woman, Angelique, who called me for coaching help because she recognized earlier than many that she'd gone down the wrong road right out of college, and she wanted to change direction before it was too late. Angelique had become an accountant because her mother had told her repeatedly while Angelique was growing up that taking professional risks or following her passion wouldn't pay the bills or help her prepare for her future. Consequently, Angelique felt like she was living her mom's best life and not her own, and she wanted to figure out what her own best life could be.

When I asked her what she'd done in her youth in her free time, Angelique talked about taking care of her stuffed animals and her own pets, running a pretend veterinary clinic in her bedroom. She'd also volunteered as an emergency worker with the local fire squad in high school, before deciding to put all of her attention in college on creating a "safe" future. She'd reluctantly chosen an accounting major, and because she was conscientious and got stellar grades, she wound up at one of the top accounting firms in the country, even earning her CPA on the first try. But every day that she got up and went to work, she knew she was doing the equivalent of putting on a costume and acting in a play. Instead of feeling alive, she didn't have a harmonious passion or even an obsessive passion. She had *no* passion, and it scared her. But when we started to talk about her enjoyment of taking care of others, I started to probe and throw out ideas to see what would happen.

"You are high in self-regulation and perseverance, which is probably why you've finished whatever you've started, regardless of whether or not it was a fit," I said. "But what if you used those same strengths to finish something really hard that's related to taking care of people instead?"

The phone went silent. I'm used to this. When you hit a nerve associated with a passion that's been squelched, people often feel like they've been punched in the gut. They're so accustomed to pushing their feelings away out of fear that zeroing in on something important has the effect of silencing them.

"You mean, like going to nursing school?" she finally breathed.

"Or medical school," I countered. "You're young. Why not?"

Everything was unlocked from that moment forward. Angelique went from having no passion to being consumed with the dream of going to nursing school. She told her live-in boyfriend that she was going to apply to a variety of schools that fit her needs and that she was going to pursue her dream instead of following him around the country as he built his own career. The relationship went through a rocky phase, but her boyfriend followed her to nursing school in Boston—and the last I heard, they were married and Angelique was blissfully happy in her work and volunteering her time as a "nurse without borders" in places around the world that needed her skills.

Angelique's story is instructive, because although she felt life was joyless, she still had passion buried inside of her that needed encouragement to come out. Rediscovering that passion led to visualization of her best possible self, an analysis of which friends and family were most supportive of her decision to upend her life, and careful goal-setting, which involved risk-taking and grit. Angelique set goals that weren't easy, but she also knew instinctively that she'd regret not pursuing those difficult goals if she didn't give them her best shot before she settled down to raise a family. As a result, the changes in her relationship status, her newfound joy and confidence, and the fact that she felt she was adding something of value to the world all added up to change her life for the better, infusing it with purpose and showing her the power of going after your dreams, even when they aren't immediately visible.

EXERCISE   Questions to ask yourself

Just like Angelique's life reboot started with a question about what she loved doing as a child, there are questions you can ask yourself if you aren't sure how to find passion in and a purpose for your own life. Try a few of these. Spend some time thinking them through and writing out your answers, and even talking to supportive family and friends who could help you brainstorm.

- Which activities, people, or places give you energy?

- Remember the Values in Action Character Strengths Survey I introduced you to earlier in the book? When you're using your top strengths in ways that bring you happiness, or that add to the happiness of others, what are you doing?

- How do you like to spend your free time?

- If you could design the perfect day for yourself, what would you do and with whom would you spend it?

- What causes do you volunteer for that matter the most to you? What about that cause is important to you?

- If you could be a superhero, what superpower would you want to have, and what would you do with it to make your life and the world better?

- If you couldn't fail, what would you be doing—or doing more of? Why?

- If you could be profiled as a CNN Hero or a person featured in NBC's *Making a Difference*, what type of difference would you be making, and why?

- What do you like to research on the computer?

- What do people compliment you on?

- When do you have fun? ■

EXERCISE   Who am I when I am at my best?

Chris Peterson, who co-created the VIA Character Strengths Survey, suggested that an equally valuable way to identify our strengths is to think of our favorite characters from history, stage, screen, literature, comic books, commercials, and anywhere else where some person, fictional or nonfictional alike, has captured our fancy. Try this approach, and write down the characters that come to mind and the strengths that you associate with them. For example, if you think of Mary Poppins, you might note her "creativity" or "zest," and if it's a historical figure such as Gandhi, you might note his "patience" or "humility." After coming up with some varied characters and their traits, write about how you have embodied those same strengths and any times when they showed you "at your best." ■

9

Happiness

I felt like I'd entered an alternate universe when I read a lengthy research paper by three of positive psychology's top luminaries—Ed Diener, Laura King, and Sonja Lyubomirsky—called "The Benefits of Frequent Positive Affect." It was the fall of 2005 when I was in the MAPP program at Penn, and I was reading more and more research that helped me to understand exactly what it takes to flourish and succeed in life. This paper, though, was a doozy, and it upended all of my previous thinking.

In one of the most profound, slam-dunk findings I've ever read, these three researchers had parsed and reviewed hundreds of studies on success in life to discover the exact opposite of what I and many others had mistakenly believed was true: we don't become happy *after* we succeed at something, but rather we succeed precisely because we are happy *first*. Their comprehensive overview of longitudinal, qualitative, correlational, and causal studies on success in friendship, health, finance, work, and all other aspects of life helped me understand why achieving certain external goals when I was younger had never made me happy for long, and had instead left me emptier than before. The grades, the awards, the schools, the scores, and the right weight never brought me the lasting satisfaction I had thought they would, and now I could see why. If I'd had access to these findings during the worst of my bulimic behavior, maybe I would have taken a different approach to my diet and health, and wouldn't have done so much damage to myself.

Since the moment I read that and other research, and learned about the power of emotional flourishing to change our lives for the better, I've made it a mission to be sure that anyone who sets and pursues goals in any area of life understands the importance of attending to their well-being as a first step toward any transformation or success. If someone were to hire me to help them become grittier in the service of pursuing a difficult goal, and I didn't share with them the importance of this finding, it would be supremely unprofessional of me. The truth is that any goal-setting of any kind has to pay attention to this fundamental fact: we greatly improve our odds of achieving goals, especially hard goals that require grit, if we start by first booting ourselves up to be our happiest, best selves.

PERMA

When I began the MAPP program, Marty Seligman's theory of well-being said that happiness consisted of having pleasure, feeling engaged in life, and leading a meaningful life. Over the next few years, as more research rolled in and more people began to weigh in on the topic, he expanded his thinking about "the well-lived life." The general understanding now is that a person who is living a flourishing life (which isn't the absence of negativity, but rather the promotion of positivity) has several different but blended activities and strengths, which go by the acronym PERMA: positive emotions, engagement, relationships, meaning, and achievements. To pump your happiness up to optimal levels, you want to pay attention to how the various components of PERMA are triggered, as well as to what you can do to create optimal conditions for goal pursuit, passion, and grit.

Positive Emotions (**P**)

Researcher Barbara Fredrickson is one of the luminaries in the field of positive psychology. Her simple question "What good are positive emotions?" yielded a pivotal theory known as "broaden and build." Her prize-winning research found that when people experience positive emotions—joy, contentment, awe, pride, love, etc.—a number of things occur that favor the continuation of the human species. They include the fact that when we broaden our awareness of our surroundings, we become more curious about other people, which in turn builds relationships. "Micromoments" of happiness—such as the joy of finding the right parking spot, feeling awe because of a thrilling experience, having our hearts fill with pride when a child does something for the first time, or feeling fulfilled because we worked our hardest to make something meaningful happen—add up to create a cushion of positivity. Fredrickson and other researchers have found that when we experience five positive emotions for every one negative emotion, we have a greater likelihood of flourishing and being proactive, purposeful, and passionate about life.

There are two ways to do this: you can either deliberately create positive emotions and micromoments through your own actions and thoughts, or you can stop and notice good things as they occur. Unhappy people have as many positive things happening around them as happy people, but the difference is that happy people deliberately salute those moments as they occur and don't let them slip by. It's been said that unhappy people don't even notice when someone holds a door for them, so be sure you don't miss a chance to celebrate the good things as they occur around you.

Engagement (**E**)

Happy people are engaged in life, and they don't experience boredom or depression as often as unhappy people. Their engagement often comes from doing things that challenge and interest them, which leads to a state of flow and the feeling that time is standing still. Whenever we are doing something and we don't notice what is happening around us, or time passes so swiftly that we can't believe a whole day has gone by, we are doing something positive that enhances our well-being and improves who we are.

The place where we are supposed to experience flow most often is at work because of the sheer number of hours so many of us spend working away from our family and friends. So if you are not engaged in your work, this could drag you down. In fact, most workers are disengaged from their work, which is predictive of low productivity, depression, and high turnover, and consultants are often brought into organizations to address this problem. One promising way to combat disengagement at work is through "job crafting," an exercise created by Justin Berg, Jane Dutton and Amy Wrzesniewski from the University of Michigan's Ross School of Business. When we can use our top strengths more directly at work—and in our personal lives—we will experience more engagement. We can also improve engagement by aligning our purpose with what we are doing.

Relationships (**R**)

One of the most powerful findings in the happiness studies is that someone cannot be designated a flourishing person without also having high-quality relationships. George Vaillant, an MD who oversaw the Harvard Grant Study for decades, found that the men who thrived emotionally into later life were the ones who cultivated and maintained positive relationships with family and friends. It led Vaillant to say conclusively, "Happiness is Love. Full stop." Chris Peterson, whom I've already mentioned was a mentor and who was one of the leading figures in positive psychology, frequently said that every finding on happiness could be boiled down to one phrase: "Other people matter."[1] Gritty people remain passionate and persevering often because they have built and maintained a team around them, and they don't just receive support but give it as well. If you want to be happy and gritty, this component of PERMA cannot be overstated.

Meaning (**M**)

Happy people don't just have lives of pleasure or engagement. They also feel that their life is meaningful and serves a higher purpose that makes the world better. Meaning can take many forms. It can come from being a loving parent, breaking barriers for others, having a skill that serves those who need it, or bringing hope to others. A meaningful life is infused with passion and purpose, so pursuing worthwhile goals with grit is an important part of what leads to flourishing in your life.

Achievement (**A**)

Some people are uncomfortable with the idea of achievement being part of a flourishing life, but that's usually because of a misperception of achievement. Achievement in PERMA isn't about winning or being number one; instead, it's about accomplishing goals that are meaningful and purposeful. Research finds that people would rather be doing something than nothing, and self-determination theory says that to thrive, people need to feel masterful in their own environments. Not all achievements will bring happiness, however. Pursuing extrinsic goals that reflect superficial desires, like money and fame, or that are someone else's dreams, doesn't result in a satisfying feeling of accomplishment or happiness. Research has also found that the happiest people wake up every day to pursue clear-cut, difficult goals that are outside their comfort zone—and not only do these goals produce the best outcomes, but they also result in the highest levels of self-esteem and self-efficacy.

Other ways happiness fuels grit

There are many other ways that emotional flourishing can improve your ability to be gritty, and one of them is making you better able to deal with physical pain. To break down prisoners and make torture more effective, captors exploit the importance of close relationships by telling prisoners that no one cares about them or is coming to save them. The subsequent feeling of abandonment amplifies the pain of physical torture. Positive emotions help people withstand torture. For our purposes, the more well-being you can create, the more easily you'll be able to cope with the physical and emotional challenges that occur when you need to exhibit grit.

New research has found that anxiety and depression can fuel procrastination because it's easier to give up when unhappiness rules our thinking. One of the best ways to deal with this is to "time travel" and imagine an important goal has been reached—instead of focusing only on the work in front of you. The research finds that the positive emotions generated by imagining a completed goal can lift a person's mood and allow them to get started on, or stick with, hard work.[2]

Wise interventions

When I entered the positive psychology field, one of the embryonic areas was called "positive interventions," which was the identification of actions that could boost a person's emotional flourishing. The list of proven interventions that worked for most people was small at that time, but ten years later, dozens of countries have produced thousands of pieces of research on what works to amplify our well-being. Now the popular terminology for this area is "wise interventions," because the need to tailor these actions to a person's strengths, talents, and interests is recognized. For example, a person like me who is high in zest and bravery will always respond favorably to physical movement and novelty, while a person who is high in self-regulation and critical thinking might do better with an intervention such as meditation.

Below, I've listed the areas of wise intervention that have the most robust research behind them and that should be considered for anyone who wants to up their well-being, life satisfaction, and outlook. How someone first responds to an intervention has been found to be predictive of whether that action will reliably work for them in the long term, so take note of the emotions you experience as you sample these and then build them into your life accordingly so that the positive emotions help you grow your grit.

Strengths use. One of the reasons my new clients take the VIA Character Strengths Survey is that identifying our top strengths has been found to improve our well-being. When you pair strengths identification with challenging yourself to use those strengths in new and creative ways to accomplish goals and interact with others—and brainstorm combining these tactics effectively—you get an even more powerful burst of energy and well-being, and the impact can last as long as one year. Some research has found that educating a group about character strengths combined with having them do rigorous physical activity resulted in both greater personal self-awareness and awareness of the strengths of others. Strengths-based interventions are also effective in increasing life satisfaction.

Gratitude. Another well-proven method to up well-being is to practice gratitude. Gratitude is one of the top character strengths associated with emotional flourishing, and one of the most publicized findings in the field of positive psychology has been about the importance of gratitude, leading to a glut of gratitude journals for purchase everywhere you turn. While noting that which you're grateful for is a useful activity, a slightly more nuanced and powerful way to practice gratitude is to list that which you are grateful for each day, as well as *why* that thing occurred in your life. When you connect your gratitude with your own proactive behavior, it's easier to see how you can generate more positive micromoments of well-being in your own life. Other popular ways to practice gratitude include a "gratitude visit," in which you write a letter of gratitude to someone you've never properly thanked, and then deliver it to them in person. More research on gratitude has found that reflecting upon any of our past challenges and reframing them with gratitude has a powerful impact on increasing happiness, reducing depression, and offering closure on difficult experiences.

Journaling. For many decades, James Pennebaker has been researching the impact of writing down one's thoughts and feelings, and he has found that keeping diaries, writing prompts, and doing similar exercises accomplish many positive things. They enhance well-being, improve immune-system function, and help create meaning in life, among many other beneficial outcomes. Newer research has found that blogging has a similarly favorable outcome, probably because getting feedback from others can be a validating experience. Learning how to write a new, positive narrative about your life instead of telling yourself the same limiting story can have a transformational effect as well. There's even research showing that writing in longhand, as opposed to using a keyboard, may offer more benefits because of the part of the brain it involves. It's also interesting to note that asking people to write about positive emotions has been related to enhancing happiness, as well as reducing illness, compared to a control group.

Spirituality. Many different strands of research have found that having a sense of spirituality adds positivity to a person's life, as long as the beliefs are not connected with narrow-minded religious practices. Specifically, believing that your faith is the only "right" way is linked to greater stress and more negative emotions, while using your faith as a positive coping tool, without judging other spiritual doctrines, is linked to greater well-being. Much research has focused on how faith-based gatherings can also offer protective benefits because of the social interaction, which often includes acts of gratitude and altruism.

Coaching. The use of a trained coach who uses evidence-based tools for change also leads to increased well-being. Research from Australia found that solution-focused coaches who met with individuals and groups about goal accomplishment between three and twenty times helped to increase people's hope, hardiness, and happiness, while also reducing their depression. Executive coaching that focuses on personal transformation and the cultivation of leadership qualities also leads to increased goal attainment, resilience, and workplace well-being, along with a reduction in disengagement and stress. Overall, coaching inter-ventions have been found to succeed in groups that vary from high school students to high-level executives, contributing to greater suc-cess, more flourishing, and less negativity.

Hope. People who are hopeless often have no goals and have stopped trying to make progress toward feeling better, so having hope is a key indicator of emotional flourishing, resilience, and striving for goal accomplishment. Hope and optimism are often tied together in the research because both are connected with seeing one's life and the world generally as a place where one can succeed and be happy. Enhanc-ing hope has been found to change thinking, which leads people to see more potential pathways to goal accomplishment as well as to believe they can carry out those solutions. People with high hope tend to per-sist longer in goal pursuit, have better outcomes, and deal with stress in more resilient ways.

Physical exercise. One of the most natural mood-boosters available is movement. Exercise enhances vitality and has long been touted as one of the best ways to clear your head, circulate oxygen and blood throughout the body, get stronger, and become fitter, but more of us need to take advantage of its natural benefits. In fact, the average American child now spends half as much time outdoors as did his counterparts in previous generations, and often spends as much as eight hours a day watching television or using a screen of some kind.

Getting our youth, as well as more adults, to exercise has long been a goal of fitness activists, but the research from positive psychology has found that exercise also has a powerful effect on the brain when it comes to reducing anxiety, depression, and hopelessness, while increasing energy, self-efficacy, and happiness.

Some research points to the value of interval training, which consists of raising one's heart rate to maximum levels for short periods, and then cycling back and forth to less vigorous levels. This type of activity not only improves fitness levels quickly and effectively, it also elevates mood for longer periods of time. Other research finds that combining physical exercise with being outdoors raises vitality levels within twenty minutes, and this lowers worry and depression as well. Hiking outdoors also boosts mental focus, creativity, memory, and self-confidence. Even better, combining meditation with aerobic exercise substantially increases the production of new brain cells in the hippocampus, reduces the ruminative tendencies associated with depression, and improves concentration and attention. Think various forms of flow and power yoga.

Altruism. The "helper's high" is what we feel when we give to others, and much research points out that when we choose to give to others, we actually gain more from the exchange than the person who received the aid. Giving to others—whether it's our time, money, or energy—can distract us from our own worries and put our struggles in perspective, particularly when we give to those less fortunate than we are. Adam Grant, the author of *Give and Take,* did a revolutionary fundraising study as an undergraduate psychology major at Harvard University. His study showed that when fundraisers were briefly exposed to gratitude from the recipients of scholarships, they spent 142 percent more time on the phone and brought in 171 percent more revenue, even when using the same sales script.[3] When we are giving, we feel more motivated, passionate, and engaged. It's also possible for the behavior to create a virtuous cycle. In U.S. states where subjective well-being is high, people are more likely to donate a kidney to strangers, and in turn, being more altruistic generates more well-being.

Meditation. I often call meditation the silver bullet of interventions because of the extraordinary number of studies that show its positive impact on rewiring the brain, as well as other innumerable positive outcomes. Loving-kindness meditation (sending positive emotions to yourself, your loved ones, and everyone else) seems to have longer-lasting outcomes for building positive emotions, improving relationships with others, and experiencing less depression than do simple mindfulness practices. Some of the most exciting research on meditation has shown specific changes in the brain, in the areas associated with self-regulation and ecstasy, and these changes come about after just a few weeks of short daily meditation practice. There are a large number of apps and websites these days to help people learn a variety of meditation techniques, and a growing number of retreats and courses exist all over the world as well to provide shared learning and experiences. It's especially interesting to note that a 2011 study found that people who meditated for eight weeks greatly improved their control of the brain rhythms that block out pain—so if you're looking for a technique to help you learn how to remain gritty when difficulties make you want to quit, meditation can be a great intervention.[4]

In the last ten years, the number of studies on how to improve well-being in evidence-based ways has skyrocketed, and these studies have underscored how amplified well-being feeds directly into success and productivity. For people who wish to become grittier, learning about how subjective well-being is tied directly into the behaviors that make persistence, zest, and mental toughness more accessible is an important step.

EXERCISE   **More ways to boost happiness**

In addition to the wise interventions I described in this chapter, here are a few more suggestions to explore, to help you find what else helps boost your happiness.

- **Check out web-based platforms such as those from Happify and the Greater Good Science Center.** They provide and update numerous articles, online courses, and audio tracks on improving well-being. They also cover a range of topics—altruism, goal-setting, grit cultivation, stress reduction, combatting negative thinking, positive parenting, and much more—and it's all from an evidence-based perspective. Take a look! Happify.com and Greatergood.berkeley.edu.

- **Eat more fruits and vegetables,** because doing so has been found to correlate with not just better health but also greater happiness. Researchers have found that eating more fruits and vegetables is predictive of experiencing higher life satisfaction and well-being—in fact, doing so has been found to produce as positive an impact as moving from unemployment to employment.[5] How about that?

- **Spend time around people who do good work**—for example, by volunteering. Professor and psychologist Jonathan Haidt says that we become "elevated" when we are in the presence of awe-inspiring behavior. It causes us to experience "tingly" and "warm" feelings within and also makes us more likely to engage in prosocial behavior ourselves.[6] A win-win dynamic!

- **Write a thank-you note to someone every week**—maybe make Thursdays "thank you Thursdays." Expressing gratitude has a huge impact on well-being, and when it becomes a habit, it will naturally lift your spirits on a regular basis.

- **Fill your calendar with planned activities to enjoy with people who uplift, energize, and fill you with positive emotions.** Happy people are often anticipating events that they know will allow them to relax, laugh, reminisce, and enjoy themselves. So plan ahead for this proven mood-booster. ■

EXERCISE   What will I not regret?

Research on regret finds that as we age, our regrets about the roads not taken and the ventures not pursued can build into a toxic and destructive mind-set that can erase zest, hope, and new goal-setting from our lives. In fact, the popular book *The Top Five Regrets of the Dying* says the number-one regret people in hospice care cite is not living *the life they wanted* to live, but instead pleasing others by taking well-worn, safe paths. To avoid this possible outcome in our own lives, we can begin by identifying the future regrets we might have if we don't give this some thought now. So, take the time now and list the top five regrets you will *not* have at the end of your life. Once you've identified these, consider and describe what it will take for you not to have those regrets. What specifically will you do to ensure that you don't end your life with "Coulda-woulda-shoulda . . . " on your lips? ■

Goal Setting

few years ago, the *New York Times* ran a front-page article about Google X, a secret division of the company in an undisclosed location, staffed by some of the most creative and resourceful robotic experts and electrical engineering geniuses they could gather. Their super-secret mission? To solve seemingly unsolvable goals, like building a staircase to the moon, designing a plate that would calculate the calories of the food on it, and creating a car that could drive itself. Their list of what could kindly be called nearly impossible goals was filled with dozens of ideas. Seven years after Google X launched, several of the goals, such as the self-driving car, have been realized.[1]

People with authentic grit are renowned for setting hard—some would say unrealistic—goals. If the goals were easy, grit wouldn't be called for. Because people with grit don't go for easy, low-hanging fruit and have to work persistently for a long time to see success, their pursuit of tough goals, and often their success in achieving them, is what inspires other people to step out of their comfort zone, too.

I want to quickly note here that just because one person's goals are difficult for them doesn't mean that that same goal will be difficult for everyone. It's the fact that you have to push yourself hard to overcome your own circumstances that matters when you are setting and pursuing your own gritty goals. After all, a working-class immigrant's goal to attend college won't present the same obstacles to someone who is born with money and academic resources, nor is the goal of changing careers as challenging for someone with a support system and a safety net if things don't work out.

Why do goals matter so much?

People with authentic grit have to have goals because that's what they are channeling their passion and energy toward. Without the goal, they run the risk of simply being overly emotional people whose energy never finds a home that lights up their lives—and inspires others. But it's important to also note that the research on goals shows that they serve a powerful purpose for everyone, which is partially why Marty Seligman put achievement as the "A" in his theory of PERMA. In his book *Flourish,* Seligman explains that achievement is an important part of living a happy life because without it, we don't ever feel masterful in our environments or in our lives. He concluded that people who accomplish outstanding achievements don't simply do them to win an award or to be famous, but that they do so because it's part of how they define themselves and find meaning in their lives.

The research on goals has found that they perform at least four critical functions:

- **Goals direct our attention, both cognitively and behaviorally, toward what matters.** Without goals, we are stimulated everywhere, all the time, without any organizing purpose, which puts us at risk of not taking advantage of opportunities to do something meaningful. As one saying goes, "Goals without feedback and feedback without goals are both meaningless." If we set no goals, we have no scorecard at the end of our lives—or even our days—to measure our progress, impact, or efforts.

- **Goals energize people, and difficult goals are more energizing than easy goals or no goals.** This energy also extends to the fact that people have more happiness when they set and pursue difficult goals, because we value and cherish what we work for, not what comes easily.

- **Goals impact persistence, and hard goals particularly impact persistence because they prolong effort.** This leads to the natural outcome that hard goals always result in better performance, whether they are assigned, self-set, or set with others.

- **Goals lead to the discovery of one's own skills and resources, while they also bring awareness to other task-relevant strategies and knowledge that need to be acquired.** When our goals call upon us to use a skill—such as reading a compass because we want to do a challenging hike, creating Excel spreadsheets to plan for the financial fitness we desire, or brushing up on swimming to get a scuba-diving certification—we immediately analyze our abilities to see if we are up to the challenge. If we are reminded of other successes, it builds confidence, and if we are new to the challenge, it pinpoints exactly what we need to learn.

The self-efficacy engine that can

"The little engine that could" demonstrates what is called self-efficacy—in other words, the engine in this story didn't know if she could accomplish the goal, but she wasn't going to stop trying and had a basic belief that she'd figure it out. This quality of believing that you have what it takes to accomplish the goals in front of you is self-efficacy, and it's part of the scholarship of Stanford University researcher Albert Bandura, who developed self-efficacy theory in the 1980s as part of the research on human motivation that helps us understand not just why people do what they do, but also how they do it.

There are several reasons why self-efficacy is necessary to cultivate grit. First, if you have self-efficacy, you are more likely to set hard goals. It's also a trait that is seen among people who are flourishing emotionally, a condition that has been found to precede all success in life. Also, people with high self-efficacy are more committed to their goals and are more likely to both start with high goals and then move on to even harder goals when they succeed.

Bandura found that there are four ways to build self-efficacy:[2]

- **Have good stress responses,** such as a regular meditation or exercise practice, the ability to use humor to lighten the mood and reframe challenges, and supportive relationships that create a positive, forgiving, and proactive community for difficult times.

- **Be near someone or have a role model who has accomplished the goal you want to accomplish** or who exhibits the behaviors you want to acquire.

- **Have a significant other who has faith in your abilities**—and because of your regard for and trust in this person, you believe in yourself, too. This person can be a spiritual guide, a grandparent, a teacher, a coach, or anyone else who has seen you in enough situations that you feel they see you in an authentic light.

- **Have mastery experiences of accomplishing smaller goals that set the stage for the accomplishment of larger goals.** This fourth way of building self-efficacy is overwhelmingly the most powerful, which serves to underscore why having any goals at all is such a potent force for good in our lives.

Another way to build self-efficacy is through listening to inspiring messages, such as those delivered by company leaders, motivational speakers, and wise elders. I watched this happen when one of my clients decided to work on his leadership skills. Rich Harris was the CEO of AddThis when he hired me to help him communicate and connect in strengths-based, positive ways. He had a long history of being a high achiever and of taking risks to change careers, such as when he decided after law school that law wasn't the right profession for him. In addition to being a resourceful entrepreneur and businessman, Rich is a competitive distance cyclist, undertaking long rides in the mountains to hone his physical and emotional toughness.

When he and I began to work together, Rich didn't rate himself highly as an inspirational leader, and he realized that if he wanted to create exciting opportunities for his company, which he was brought into to turn around, he was going to need to emotionally connect with the employees with passion in an urgent call to action. When he arrived at AddThis, Rich described the workforce as having "blissful ignorance . . . they work hard but don't have to make tough choices, so many perceive themselves as successful." He explained that he'd inherited some terrific people whom he had to challenge—some for the first time—to set and pursue big goals, and that he'd have to remake himself as a leader in some of the ways he was asking others to dig deeper and do riskier, harder things.

I introduced Rich to the concept of grit, and together we crafted messages that he honed, practiced, and delivered to tremendous acclaim. Within months, AddThis was leaner and more focused, and employees were knocking profits out of the ballpark. Rich led the organization through a successful merger with Oracle, and after its conclusion, he was moved by the emails and messages from people in the company who said that his town-hall meetings had become the highlight of their work lives, and that he had managed to infuse so much honesty, positivity, resilience, and emotion into the addresses that people believed in themselves and their strengths in new ways, which allowed them to work with greater energy, focus, and passion.

Rich is the textbook example of a leader who had grit personally, but who managed to transform himself into someone who didn't just embody it, but who also found a way to connect with hundreds of people in such a powerful way that he altered their self-belief for the better. Rich is a true transformational leader, and when people are fortunate enough to work with someone like him, they can build their self-efficacy and start the journey to tackling their own hard goals and developing authentic grit, too.

Intrinsic goals: "The stove is running hot"

Gritty people are fueled with an intensity that borders on ferocity when it comes to accomplishing their goals, which separates them from people who don't set their own goals and who aren't lit up with a desire to do something important to them. One of the first rules in the world of goal-setting science and emotional thriving is that the goal has to pass what I call the "So what then?" test. I often challenge people with, "So what then?" As I've already mentioned, when my clients first tell me about their goals, I respond with this question because I need to understand what is driving them—why they want to put their strengths, resources, time, and pride on the line. If they are setting a goal for the wrong reasons, a satisfying answer to this question will be difficult for them.

Katie Ledecky, the international swimming phenomenon and five-time Olympic gold medalist, grew up around the corner from me, in a family that was custom-made for this superstar to evolve into the goal-setting machine she has become. In a town where some parents have been known to videotape their children's practices starting at a young age in a feverish focus on their hoped-for greatness, Ledecky's parents have always been remarkably unruffled by what began to take shape while Katie was just a young, always-smiling girl in Catholic elementary school.

At swim practices where we and other parents spent many hours on hard benches and folding chairs, Katie's mom, Mary Gen, was always upbeat about everything and everyone, especially about the recipes she found in magazines and shared with me. I found her personality to be so remarkably optimistic and winning that I submitted an essay about her to my professors at Penn called "The Happiest Person I Know." And I remember the day before Katie left for the 2012 Olympic Trials meet, which would launch her to greatness. My Masters team was practicing in the pool next to the lane where Katie was doing solitary laps as her coach logged her splits. Katie's father, Dave, who was sitting in a glassed-in area above the pool, never once looked up from his newspaper during Katie's warm-up, though the rest of us tried to steal looks at her stroke underwater. If either parent ever felt their daughter was more important or special than her own brother or that they were personally invested in her success, it was never apparent.

There's no question that Katie's goals are hers alone. She is completely self-motivated and wouldn't churn through the water before and after school, on weekends, and on holidays just because someone else was making her do it. The sport is simply too difficult to sustain the effort it demands, and the workload usually weeds out less motivated swimmers by puberty if it's not their own passion. In fact, I was walking our dog to the neighborhood park one day about ten years ago when I encountered Mary Gen outside. She knew about my work with goal-setting so she asked me what I thought about something she had found in Katie's room: "want" goals, which were beyond the expected goals for her young age.

"What do you think?" she asked, almost in bemusement. "Is this normal?"

Although aspects of Katie's personality are inscrutable, and her mature approach to hard work and goals are exceptional among American youth, much of what she does to be at a superstar level isn't flashy or unavailable to others. Part of the "secret" to her success is that she shows up at workouts and does her best on a daily basis, something that sounds easy, but in reality is not—and when she is asked how she swims so fast, her advice is simple: set hard goals.[3] What does appear to set her apart, and what I see in other gritty people, is the degree of the insatiable intensity she infuses into her goals, and that fuels her passion to take swimming where no woman has ever taken it before. Coaches have commented on the mysterious "fury" that emerges from this modest and respectful young woman when she is in the water, saying in awe, "The stove is running hot."[4]

Goal-setting theory: "learning goals" and "performance goals"

I'd never heard of the science of goal-setting theory until I began the MAPP program with Marty Seligman. Like many other people, by the time I reached Penn I'd read and reread the bestselling self-help books on goals: those that advocated for conditions proven effective by "The Harvard Study of 1950" (the members of that class who wrote down their goals had an exceptionally high percentage of accomplishments); SMART goals (Specific, Measurable, Action-Oriented, Realistic, and Time-Sensitive goals, which do not inspire us the way others' "unrealistic"—read gritty—goals do); and even the Law of Attraction (if you want it, think about it with enough passion, imagine what it would feel like to already have it, and then you will get it), among others.

I thought these were the time-tested and proven ways to set and accomplish goals. Many were presented as "studies," which certainly masquerade as real research if you aren't savvy enough to challenge them. And the truth is, I was slightly suspicious that you could get what you desire simply by wanting it badly enough, even though I had the experience of writing down my future vision of my life, in 1985, and realized in the late 1990s that much of it had come true. So I had an open mind about the fact that you might not always be able to understand how your dreams come true and that certain things happen that appear to be "magical."

One of my first assignments in the MAPP program was about goal-setting theory. Gary Latham and Edwin Locke had proved through hundreds of studies that best performance always occurs when someone sets specific and challenging goals. As I dug deeper, I learned that goal-setting theory distinguishes between two types of goals: learning goals and performance goals. *Learning goals* describes conditions in which the person doesn't have a history of pursuing this type of goal and so has no idea how long it will take, or even what strategies need to be used, to succeed. Since this person is new to the task, and may not have the necessary skills to succeed quickly or at all, it's acceptable to tell themselves or hear others coach them to "do your best."

But even if it is a learning situation, Locke and Latham found that setting higher learning goals leads to better performance than setting a mediocre learning goal. A simple example would be the difference between learning how many U.S. presidents there have been versus learning the names and backgrounds of all the presidents. *Performance goals* also benefit from being challenging and specific, attributes that are the wheelhouse of gritty people, who wouldn't think of setting anything other than a very difficult goal with distinct metrics and a clear finish line.

Most people, however, are languishing and not "flourishing," which means that they don't set these types of goals. They shoot for "low goals" or "no goals," which are the two other types of goals we can set. When we set low goals, however, we easily reach those goals, but we won't be satisfied because we didn't stretch to get there. Gary Latham says that most people set these types of goals because they don't want to disappoint themselves or look bad in their own eyes, but the irony is that the research shows it's only by going outside our comfort zone in pursuit of hard goals that we build "authentic self-esteem," which cannot be wished or hoped into existence.

Louise's story

When we don't know the difference between these types of goals, we run the risk of developing "stubborn grit," which will hurt us in the long run and won't result in excellence. I saw this occur with a client of mine who had a stellar work background, with lots of responsibility and a history of managing people successfully, but who transitioned out of the corporate world and into entrepreneurship thinking that the same type of hard work that had propelled her to senior leadership would stand her in good stead in the new company she had created.

When Louise started to work with me, she was discouraged and had begun to lose the confidence and passion that had been her personality trademark for years. She shared that she didn't know what she was doing wrong and needed a coach to help her figure it out—or she'd lose her company and millions of dollars. She was sure that she'd put herself in the best possible situation to succeed as far as goal-setting and accountability, so she was especially troubled that nothing was working out the way she wanted it to.

I immediately spotted the problem when Louise explained her system to me. She started her week with a sunrise call on Monday morning with other business leaders, who shared their week's goals with one another. On Friday morning, the same group members reported back to one another on how they had done with their goals.

Louise told me about the types of goals she usually set: pay all vendors by Wednesday night; make ten new sales by Thursday; develop an employee handbook; compare health insurance plans; and so on. She said that she almost always reported back by Friday morning that she hadn't achieved the goals she'd set for herself. She was now starting to skip the Friday-morning calls because she felt like such a failure.

I asked her a simple question: "Have you ever before done any of the goals you are setting for yourself in this business?"

She thought for a moment, and then said, "No. This is all new. I always had a secretary, a staff, and people to call upon when I needed to get something done in my old company. Plus, I knew what I was doing. I'm in way over my head now, and I have no idea how to dig out."

Louise's problem was clear. She had almost nothing but learning goals because she'd never been an entrepreneur before. She'd never written an employee handbook before, never booked sales on sales calls before, and so on. Yet Louise was marking all of these goals as performance goals and giving herself arbitrary deadlines because she felt she "should" be able to accomplish them if she worked hard enough. But without previous experience, a staff to lean on, or anyone to provide her with step-by-step methods to break her goals down into manageable steps, Louise was flailing and failing. And the worse she felt, the more she isolated herself in embarrassment, ensuring that no one would be available to mentor her in the right ways.

Once I explained that she wasn't a business dud but had mistaken learning goals for performance goals and that there were solutions to her problems she could implement immediately, Louise's confidence and spirits rose immediately. She started to understand that having a "do your best" deadline and expectation while she learned the ropes was going to be the best way for her to gauge her performance, and she focused on brainstorming as many solutions as possible to her challenges first and then experimenting with ways to proceed that matched her strengths and time. I also suggested that she immediately get a mentor to flatten her learning curve and help her come up with tested metrics that could allow her to turn some of her learning goals into performance goals more quickly.

If you want the inspiring, uplifting, and positive outcomes associated with authentic grit, it's imperative to understand the differences between the learning-goal and performance-goal orientations so that you don't misspend the time, energy, focus, and perseverance you will need to succeed at your hard goals. In my experience, this is one of the primary problems people and organizations make, and that can send anyone into a downward spiral of misery, confusion, and failure. The good news is that it is also very fixable with the right knowledge and commitment to learning how to apply goal-setting research for best results.

The importance of accountability

One of the biggest mistakes people make when pursuing goals is that they fail to build in the accountability that will help ensure they do what they say they need to do. The reason people don't do this is they falsely assume that the goal is so important to them that they will have no trouble hitting their deadlines. This mistake happens with the full gamut of goals, whether it be engaging in physical exercise, remaining committed to a cause, changing life circumstances, or saving money. If change were easy, everyone would do it. Part of the reason why change is so hard is that our daily lives are filled with people, circumstances, and temptations that can undermine our commitments. Gritty people set up accountability in a variety of ways.

Accountability can take the form of a coach, like me, who is paid to help guide you, brainstorming and meeting with you, in person or virtually, to ensure that progress is made and that setbacks prompt new strategies. Mentors can also serve as accountability figures, offering ideas or strategies that have worked for them, while holding your feet to the fire to make sure you do your work. Sports coaches provide workouts, feedback, and team-training opportunities for gritty athletes with big goals.

Sometimes setting up accountability is as simple as partnering with a peer or a friend, or a group of friends. This is what my daughter Samantha did when she prepared for the LSATs, which is the standardized test required for law school applications in the United States. She and a friend who had the same goal studied and often took LSAT practice tests together; Samantha wound up taking fourteen in all to help get her best possible score. The hard work paid off, because Samantha got into every law school she applied to, including Harvard, which she currently attends. Although my daughter possesses passion and talent, it was her hard work—sealed with accountability to peers—that put her over the top and helped her proceed toward her eventual dream of becoming a public defender.

Mastermind groups, too, have always had a place in the list of successful strategies that help people achieve their goals. I have helped to start mastermind groups that meet in person as well as online, and both have played powerful roles in assisting me to move forward in my personal and professional life with some of my hardest goals. Part of the benefit of a mastermind group is the social support it provides in the form of friendships that go past superficial niceties, allowing you to be emotionally vulnerable, as well as hopeful and jubilant, all of which will come into play when your goals are outside your comfort zone and the obstacles are daunting.

When I was writing *Creating Your Best Life* in 2008 and I made the difficult decision to temporarily close my coaching practice to move to a secluded location to write, it was my mastermind group that encouraged me to take the difficult steps that carried big risks and possible financial losses. They challenged me to outline exactly what I would do on a daily basis, offered support of all kinds (technology assistance, check-in calls, driving my children to sports practices, and much more), and even made me laugh when I was miserable and afraid I'd bitten off more than I could chew. I never could have written that book without their help, and I firmly believe that everyone can benefit from such a group. When a mastermind group is run with specific guidelines and the right people are included (people who are enthusiastic about change and who want to support others in doing the same), its members will stay on track and avoid turning the meetings into a complaining session or litany of woes.

There are other forms of accountability that make a big difference. Some people broadcast their goals publicly—through a website, mass email, or social media—and some have the ability to go on the mainstream media and do the same, if they have access to that type of platform. I've run large groups in organizations and school settings where people are invited to share their goals with the group, and I've seen that type of public support be transformational. Not everyone wants to be, or should be, this public, but when the context is supportive and caring, publicly stating your goals can result in friends and colleagues checking in on you, asking how you're progressing, and supplying you with support and enthusiasm to keep you going when you are tempted to quit.

Writing down goals drives commitment

There is evidence that writing down your goals enhances commitment. This can take the form of publicly posting your goals on a website or in a blog, creating "behavioral contracts," and journaling. The exercise "Best Possible Future Self," which involves writing down where you envision yourself in ten years, has been found to prompt goal-directed thinking and to also clarify goals in conflict, while raising optimism and evoking persistence.

In 2015, National Public Radio aired a story called "The Writing Assignment That Changes Lives"[5] that covered an online goal-setting and journaling program that is having an impressive impact on university students when it comes to their retention in school and their grade-point averages. Jordan Peterson, who teaches in the department of psychology at the University of Toronto, launched a curriculum called Maps of Meaning, which walks students through questions that help them identify their motivation, plans for the future and specific goals, and the strategies they will use to help them overcome any setbacks. He divides the expressive writing combined with the goal-setting into two sections: "past authoring" and "future authoring."

One study at McGill University in Montreal found that at-risk students who took the Maps of Meaning course were less likely to drop out and more likely to improve academic performance. Another study on what happened to students who took the course in their freshman year found that the writing exercises erased nearly all the differences between gender and race. The course is now offered at the Rotterdam School of Management in the Netherlands as well, and the results are especially powerful there because of the proliferation of immigrants who might be vulnerable to "stereotype threat." Peterson feels a goal-setting intervention that keeps such students in school is life changing: "You don't have to be a genius to get through school. You don't even have to be that interested. But zeroes are deadly."[6]

EXERCISE   Ways to set better goals

- **Make a bucket list of goals, including a list of those you have already accomplished so that you can prime the pump of feeling masterful.** Some people like to shoot for a hundred, but the number is less important than generating a list to get you going. Exchange lists with other people you invite to join you in this exercise, and explain to one another the "So what then?" behind your goals.

- **If you already have some goals that you want to accomplish but you feel stuck, try the Five Whys approach to get to the heart of why you may not be moving forward.** The Five Whys is an exercise that also helps with problem-solving, which is why you'll find it at the end of chapter 11.

- **One great way to make yourself accountable for your goals is to schedule emails that will be delivered to you in the future,** reminding you of steps you need to take and why your goal is so important, and challenging you to remain committed. At the website futureme.org, you can create emails that will be sent to you in upcoming weeks, months, and even years, assuming your email address won't change. Not only is this a great strategy for accountability, it also doesn't cost a penny.

- **New research finds that people who consciously think about the goals they need to accomplish during the day and how these fit into longer-term goals and plans are less emotionally exhausted, more satisfied at work, and even have a happier commute to work!**[7] So in the morning, as you think through your day's activities and about how and when you will accomplish them, also ask yourself where they fit into your longer-term plans. This type of thinking is known as "goal-directed prospection," and it will create more positive emotions, enhance self-regulation, and give you a leg up when you set about your work in a goal-directed state of mind. ■

EXERCISE   Meet me in ten years

One of the best-known writing exercises to emerge from the field of positive psychology is "Best Possible Future Self," which I have referred to earlier in this book. Now is a good time for you to engage in this exercise in earnest, if you haven't already. This journaling exercise consists of spinning yourself ten years into the future and writing about this future self for twenty minutes a day, three days in a row. You want to explore as many avenues and areas of your life as possible in each writing session:. Where do you live? How do you spend your time? Who is with you? How do you interact with your friends and family? Are there causes you support? What risks have you taken that have paid off? After your third day of writing, spend an additional ten minutes writing an introduction about this person—your future self—as if you're presenting this person to an audience.

   Research has found that doing this writing exercise boosts zest and optimism, clarifies conflicting goals, evokes self-compassion, and promotes proactive goal-attainment behavior.[8] ■

11

Self-Regulation

n 2014, Michael Lewis, bestselling author of *The Big Short, Liar's Poker,* and *Moneyball,* among many other books, pulled the curtain back on what life was like in the White House in his profile of President Barack Obama. For months, he traveled on Air Force One, hung around in briefings, and played basketball with Obama, and during this time he learned how some of the findings of social psychology were being used to streamline and maximize the president's effectiveness. Among the most important: Obama made no decisions that he didn't need to make, so he wore only blue or gray suits, ate what was served to him, and allowed other people to take over the mundane details of his life, from sock selection to where to be at what time.

Obama did this to preserve his decision-making energy because of recent findings on willpower that show that effortful decisions use up willpower, creating something called "decision fatigue." "You need to routinize yourself," Lewis explained. "You can't be going through the day distracted by trivia."[1]

Obama did a few things that everyone who wants grit needs to learn how to do. He didn't waste time wondering if he should do something that didn't really matter a great deal; instead, he delegated those tasks to other people. He created routines that trigger automatic behaviors and thereby conserved emotional energy. When he had to focus on huge issues about which only a president could decide, he brought a clear mind and high-quality focus to the problem at hand.

Saying "no" says "yes"
to the right things later in life

Remember my mention earlier in the book of Walter Mischel's famous marshmallow experiment, in which preschool children who could delay eating a marshmallow for fifteen minutes were later found to be more likely to have high SAT scores, fewer behavioral issues, more leadership qualities, more popularity, higher grades, and fewer addictions than the kids who couldn't say no to temptation? More research has found that this early delaying ability predicts even more positive outcomes, including fewer divorces, more job tenure, and greater happiness. Mischel is now looking into whether this ability also predicts higher income as an adult, which he suspects it does.

Policymakers and education reformers also stress the importance of teaching self-control at young ages. A report released by the National Bureau of Economic Research in 2015 said that non-cognitive skills like grit and self-regulation are at least as important, if not more so, than any knowledge that workers bring to the workplace, and that those skills ought to be a key focus in elementary school because of the "malleable" nature of personality at that age.[2] Cal Newport, the author of the bestselling *Deep Work: Rules for Focused Success in a Distracted World*, goes further in his assertion that self-regulation is a critical life skill now: "The IQ of the 21st century is the ability to focus."[3]

When I first learned about the research on self-regulation and what that quality predicts, I guiltily thought back to my children's youth, when I didn't always make them wait for rewards. I can say with certainty that if I could go back and raise my children again, this is what I would focus on most because when you can learn to delay gratification—and it is a learnable skill—it results in a cascade of positive outcomes. The research very clearly shows that people with high self-regulation don't just succeed with their goals, they also enjoy ancillary benefits like greater confidence, more friends, and amplified well-being.

Mischel's marshmallow study found that the students who did the best were the ones who essentially removed all temptation to think about the marshmallow from their consciousness: they put their heads down, turned their back on the marshmallow, sang songs to distract

themselves, and did whatever they could to keep t
marshmallow. This isn't unlike Obama's carefully c
ing him to think only about what he has to think
moment "trivia" and distractions appear, his valu
willpower is lessened, one drip at a time.

For me to overcome my bulimia, I instinctively learned to do exactly what the four-year-old "delayers" in Mischel's study did. I didn't go to any restaurants that served foods I had once binged on. Our kitchen didn't have any tempting foods that would cause me to even think about abandoning my recovery. And I usually packed lunches for work that removed the distraction of wandering into the food court at the mall and seeing a huge variety of foods I could eat. KISS, or "Keep it simple, stupid," was the acronym that worked for me; it was one that I often heard in my twelve-step program, and the more I've learned about the research on self-regulation, the more I understand that keeping decisions simple is what any of us need to do to avoid abusing our willpower.

What is willpower, anyway?

In the last fifteen years, the research on self-regulation has been vibrant and even controversial at times. One of the leaders in the field is Roy Baumeister, a bearded professor at Florida State University, who has collaborated with others to theorize that willpower probably behaves just like a muscle. Baumeister thinks that we wake up every morning with a finite supply of the ability to say "no" to ourselves and to delay gratification, and as we go through each day, we deplete that supply a little bit at a time. These "effortful" decisions involve making trade-offs in our minds about what we can and can't do.

Let's look at how this fact impacts judges who make parole decisions. In one well-known study, it was found that at the start of their workday, judges were able to assess complicated situations to determine appropriate parole decisions, but as the morning wore on, they were unable to sustain this ability.[4] Their brains became "fatigued" and defaulted to the easiest possible choice, which was whatever decision they were most accustomed to making. But after lunch, their decision-making abilities were again as sharp as they'd been at the beginning of the day, leading to the determination that taking a break and putting nutrients—particularly glucose—into the body brought willpower stores back up to full strength.

Some of the newest research on self-regulation finds that if you wholeheartedly believe you have unlimited amounts of willpower, your body will respond with heightened self-control. Sleep, laughter, and being in the presence of other people practicing willpower have also been found to bring depleted willpower back up to full strength.[5] And what's the number-one way to deplete willpower? Alcohol, it turns out—it removes our ability to say no to ourselves regarding anything, from more alcohol to food, sex, spending money, indulging in anger, and other kinds of self-destructive behavior.

Sobriety and grit

Karlyn Pipes is one of the most decorated swimmers of our time. As a child, she found early success in the pool; as a teen, she was considered one of the best up-and-coming swimmers in the country, which led to fifteen full scholarship offers, finally settling at the University of Arkansas. Karlyn's burgeoning problem with alcohol, though, resulted in her losing her scholarship and her hope of becoming an Olympian. She returned to California in shame, continuing to drink in escalating amounts until she bottomed out in her early thirties.

Getting sober gave Karlyn her life back, and her old passion for swimming roared to life again, giving her newfound purpose. She returned to college and started to swim competitively again, becoming the oldest person to win an NCAA Division II title—in fact, she won three of them and became the oldest person—at age 35—to set and hold an NCAA record. She went on to set, break, and reset over 200 FINA Masters world records. In 2015, she was inducted into the International Swimming Hall of Fame and published her memoir of recovery, *The Do-Over.*

Karlyn's story of passion being drowned by alcohol and then resurfacing upon sobriety is one that we hear and see regularly. As

Baumeister has found, alcohol is a key reason why people lose their way in life. Being gritty about anything while drinking abusively is impossible. Sometimes clients will confess to me their struggles with alcohol because they know it stands in the way of their being successful. When they can abstain from alcohol, they always find that a better, happier life is waiting for them. So although most people drink responsibly, for those for whom alcohol is a dangerous liability, I always suggest they consider stopping for the duration of our work together, if not longer, and even try an Alcoholics Anonymous meeting to see if the stories resonate and inspire them.

"The problem that has no name 2.0"

In the early 1960s, middle-aged women were found to be suffering in untold numbers from depression, hopelessness, and prescription-pill abuse, living lives of quiet desperation in the American suburbs, where raising children and using the newest vacuum wasn't enough to make them feel happy. Betty Friedan brought this issue into public view when she called it "the problem that has no name" in *The Feminine Mystique*.

I began to notice something unusual in the last few years that worried me and caused me to write about what I call "the problem that has no name 2.0." Over the past decade, middle-aged women have skyrocketed to the top of many lists of demographics that are engaging in self-destructive behaviors—behaviors that include depression, suicide attempts, eating disorders, prescription-pill abuse, and alcoholism.[6] Instead of joining the rest of the world in living longer, healthier lives, middle-aged white women are also now doing something that no other group is doing—dying earlier.[7]

I am concerned that my peer group is facing so many emotional and physical challenges at a time when being gritty has never been more important. They are struggling to deal with their disappointments, changing circumstances, and fears by succumbing to self-destructive behaviors and negative thinking, all of which undermine resilience, finding a passion and purpose, goal-setting, and building positive relationships. Their hopeless behaviors undercut self-regulation, which is a primary driver in the pursuit of hard goals. I've noticed among female clients and friends that locking on to a fresh purpose and feeling freer to launch a reinvented self later in life can have a galvanizing impact on hope and happiness, which can also reinvigorate a marriage and family.

Couples who transition successfully from one stage to another can help each other in the cultivation of self-regulation by invoking "the Michelangelo effect." When we have future goals for ourselves and share them with our partners, we are more likely to thrive, have willpower, and succeed if our partners "sculpt" us with their feedback and praise. For example, the wife who wants to re-enter the working world after staying home to raise children for fifteen years will flourish more readily if her husband sculpts her with praise for her efforts to network, learn new skills, and shuck off household tasks, instead of praising her for behaviors that don't connect with her future self, such as the taste of her meatloaf or her scrapbooking talents.

Researcher Laura King has found that divorced women and mothers of special-needs children can benefit from a writing exercise called "Lost Possible Selves," which involves writing a detailed essay about the woman you thought you'd be as you grew older, but who you will never be because of changed circumstances, such as divorcing the partner you thought you'd grow older with or raising a child who won't do the things you envisioned while you were pregnant with him or her. King found that many women are unknowingly held back by these "possible selves," and that creating detailed descriptions of the life you'll never have and bidding it farewell can break the emotional logjam.[8]

Why are so many poor people fat?

Some of the newest research on self-regulation gives me a different, more intellectual understanding of—and a lot more empathy and less judgment toward—people who are juggling the competing pressures of lots of bills and scant financial resources. Since willpower is a limited resource that is used up little by little with every effortful decision made during the day, imagine what it is like when you are struggling to get by and have to decide whether to pay the electric bill, buy groceries, or put shoes on your children's feet. When you live like this in an unending way, what do you think occurs at the end of the day? You undoubtedly overdo it, possibly with food, alcohol, or losing your temper, which could explain some of the obesity, substance abuse, and violence that is all too common among the poor.

After I did a public webinar about grit for Happify when we launched the "Grow Your Grit" track, I received many emails from people in these types of limited circumstances—people who have big dreams but worry that they don't have enough grit to get there. After reading about their economic burdens, physical challenges, and inability to get ahead, I wrote back to tell them that I think they *do* have grit but that they are probably worn down by the daily obstacles they have to cope with. I explained the science of self-regulation and encouraged them first to create habits that will preserve their mental strength and improve their physical health, and then to focus on small, winnable goals that will help them build momentum. Once they can experience the benefits of living in a way that takes advantage of the social psychology research, my hope is that these challenged low-income champions might approach their day the way Obama approached his days in the White House: with dignity, calm, and as much confidence and focus as possible. If they can do that, they have a chance of building the type of authentic grit that can help them create more of the life they really want.

Happify vs. Pokémon GO

Two of the newest visionaries in the field of positive psychology are Ofer Leidner and Tomer Ben-Kiki. After serving in the Israeli military, where they learned to work with computers that could do just about anything, they founded a company called iPlay, which they now admit contributed to a lot of procrastination and anxiety in the world by getting people hooked on games that distract them from life. After cashing out of their company, they longed to do something more meaningful with their knowledge and time. When they found the field of positive psychology, they came across the perfect way to take their skills and create something they felt the world needed. Happify is the brainchild they share with fellow tech whiz Andy Parsons; the trio has used their knowledge to hook people on the dozens of "tracks" they offer via the website and app, all of which teach users how to notice positive emotions, experience gratitude, find awe in everyday life, and combat negative thoughts. Contrast this with the fads that do nothing but distract people—like Pokémon GO—and that don't help to build grit, and you can see how important it is to keep your wits about you and get hooked only on the things that actually result in positive outcomes.

ADT—Attention Deficit Trait

In 2005, Edward Hallowell wrote an article for *Harvard Business Review* entitled "Overloaded Circuits: Why Smart People Underperform." As a psychiatrist who had helped many people diagnose and deal with attention deficit hyperactivity disorder (ADHD) and its cousin, attention deficit disorder (ADD), he was noticing the epidemic of a new, related disorder that he calls Attention Deficit Trait (ADT). Unlike ADD and ADHD, which are rooted in genetics and often come with creative, insightful gifts that can be masked by the inability to focus at times, ADT doesn't come with any gifts and is the result of living and working in a hyperkinetic world, where there are so many data points to keep track of that our brains suffer from overload and begin to shut down.

The inability to self-regulate because of the incessant use of technology, the urgent need for speed, and the inability of many to step away and recalibrate, are part of what I believe is contributing to the lack of grit in the world today. Hallowell believes that part of what causes ADT to flourish is the survival mechanism of fear, which springs into action whenever we feel startled or threatened. He writes, "In survival mode, the manager is robbed of his flexibility, his sense of humor, his ability to deal with the unknown. He desperately wants to kill the metaphorical tiger."

Hallowell is careful to make a distinction between the
he has studied. ADD and ADHD can be confirmed by
and the selective use of stimulants. ADT, which is neither of the two,
will only get better by changing a person's external environment and
responses to stress. His advice to defeat ADT and learn how to cultivate self-regulation—so that you can work toward the accomplishment
of important goals without nonstop distraction and disruption—is
similar to the wisdom on creating optimal conditions for flourishing:
promote positive emotions, remain physically connected with people
you like and respect, take care of your brain with the right rest and
nutrition, exercise your body, declutter your day and your environment to avoid distraction, and know how to self-soothe when you get
anxious so that you can return to a state of calm.

The words in our environments

Not only is our environment lying in wait with deliberate ways to disrupt us and destroy our self-regulation, there are also random, unforeseen
events that can do so, and we need to be on guard. Researchers have
found that we are constantly at the mercy of "non-conscious primes,"
which can be words, songs, places, pictures, or even people, and encoun-
tering these primes can cause us to involuntarily think and behave in
positive or negative ways. Some companies harness the positive power of
words by naming conference rooms around values the company espouses,
or behaviors they want to see among employees. Sprinklr, for example,
has conference rooms with such names as "Gratitude," "Courage," and
"Integrity." The founder, Ragy Thomas, sagely notes, "It would be kind of
hard to be arrogant in a room named Humility, wouldn't it? Or give up
in a room named Perseverance, wouldn't it?"[9]

Much attention has been paid to the types of words used in songs,
and British researchers note that the rise in alcohol-related diseases in
recent decades mirrors the increased use of positive phrases about drinking alcohol in songs during the same period.[10] And new research has
found that if we pass by a group in conversation and unwittingly hear
words like "cannot do it" or "fail," it lessens our ability to self-regulate.[11]

There's no question that having enough willpower to delay gratification so that goal pursuit and goal accomplishment are more likely—particularly when it is a long, hard road to the finish line—is exceptionally important. This is why so many people start the road to getting grit by upping their self-regulation. Fortunately, an abundance of research and new information on ways to build the willpower muscle have given us many exercises to choose from, as well as the hope that anyone can get better.

EXERCISE **Ways to improve self-regulation**

- **Return to old-school guidelines for self-discipline.** Some
  of the exercises and rules in Catholic schools, such as
  "sit up straight" and "write your sentences one hundred
  times in perfect cursive," are now actually considered
  good training for building self-discipline that spills into
  other areas of life. Pick something simple and specific to
  practice repeatedly and deliberately to build this quality.
  Paying attention to the details has also been found to be
  at the core of Special Forces training. Any inattention
  to detail can result in harm to one's self or others, so
  military training emphasizes simple and specific details
  such as shining one's shoes and making sure no threads are
  hanging off one's uniform.

- **Ask yourself questions.** While self-affirmations can,
  overall, help people achieve their goals, research finds that
  asking ourselves questions about whether or not we will
  do something specific leads to better results. So instead of
  "I will sign up for the triathlon," change it to "Will I sign
  up for the triathlon?" James Pennebaker, professor and
  chair of the Department of Psychology at the University
  of Texas at Austin, says that our social-cognitive ideas are

relevant to real-world behaviors. In other words, we need to pay attention to the way words influence us to develop (or not) the character strengths we need to be proactive and successful.

- **Choose your coffee shop carefully.** Like so many other behaviors, self-regulation and remaining on task are contagious. Whether we begin to unconsciously mimic people's breathing rate, body posture, or talking, being around people who are working hard creates a positive ripple effect. Some theories also posit that when we work in front of other people, we evoke the "audience effect," which means that we have more self-control when we believe we are being watched. Another theory is that small groups of people all doing the same thing may begin to compete with one another to achieve the best results. But regardless of why it works, remember that gritty people know how to self-regulate, and being around people who do this can be instrumental in building that habit for yourself.

- **If you're a dad, spend time playing with your kids.** This suggestion is an opportunity for dads and those who may one day be dads to foster self-regulation in their children. Several unique pieces of research tie a father's interaction with his children to their ability to self-regulate. Brigham Young University followed 325 families for several years and found that two-parent homes with fathers who demonstrated authoritative parenting developed greater numbers of children who could stick with a task and finish a project. Another key piece of research found that the quality of a father's play, most notably roughhousing, helps small children learn how to cope with feelings of frustration: in a safe environment with dad, they are able to cope through laughter.[12] ■

EXERCISE   **The five whys**

In 2011, *Harvard Business Review* ran an article on the famous Toyota Production System, a process that resulted from investigating why things don't get completed on time, or at all in some circumstances.[13] Toyota's productivity challenge is very clear and helps managers decide which projects get priority, how to eliminate waste, and which techniques produce the best results. Similarly, for anyone who wishes to develop grit, understanding which choices bring the best results and how to stop doing things that impede goal completion is essential.

So think about something you are not doing well, or at all, that you want to change. An example might be getting control of your spending to save enough to invest in something that will impact your success. Next, ask yourself, "Why is that so? Why haven't I been [fill in the blank]?" Not only do you want to identify the reason(s), you also want to examine the reason(s) by continuing to ask "Why is that so?"—until you have at least five whys shedding light on the issue. Back to our example, the inquiry could go something like this: "I don't have enough money because I can't control my spending. I can't control my spending because I have last-minute bills that wipe out my reserve. I have last-minute bills because I wait until the last second to pay. I wait until the last second to pay because my fixed expenses eat up most of my paycheck. I have so many fixed expenses because . . . ." I think you now get the idea. It's this kind of persistent inquiry that will allow you to discover the root of your problem *and* where you can begin to make the changes that will have a positive domino effect. ■

12

Risk-Taking

One of my favorite questions in my coaching practice is "What is the biggest risk you've ever taken, and what was the reward?" Inevitably people share stories of quitting jobs without a safety net, asking someone to marry them, taking a trip to a far-flung destination on a whim, and leaving graduate school in spite of investing time and money in that education. Their voices change as they talk about the variety of positive outcomes, which include fulfilling a long-held passion to enter an intriguing field, changing their worldview to become more compassionate, and throwing off the yoke of family or cultural expectations to find greater self-acceptance and sense of purpose.

People with authentic grit are not wildly unrealistic about their competencies, but they do take risks because they have self-efficacy—they believe they will figure out whatever they need to know or do to accomplish their goals. One of their most distinguishing characteristics, however, is that they do not fear failure, and they don't necessarily allow themselves to visualize or accept the idea that they will fail.

Katie Ledecky exploded onto the international swimming scene at the age of fifteen when she won the 2012 London Olympics in the 800-meter freestyle. Although she had never swum in an international meet, it didn't play havoc with her nerves. She took on the world record holder, British swimmer Rebecca Adlington, in the middle of the pool in the finals, leading wire-to-wire as the commentators sputtered disbelief. Later, Ledecky admitted that she'd never envisioned herself anywhere but at the top of the Olympic podium, despite her youth and lack of elite racing experience. The coach who guided her in subsequent years to a number of world records explained her mind-set this way: "Katie isn't afraid of failure, but failure isn't an option."[1]

The reason grit requires skillful risk-taking is that gritty people often break new ground, doing things that haven't been done by them or, often, by anyone else. They have to go outside their comfort zone over and over to get where they want, all the while with no guarantee of success. That doesn't stop them, though; they'd rather bet on themselves than accept a life in which they'll never know what might have been.

Our best life calls for risks

In 2008, I was interviewed by the *New York Times* for an article about bucket lists that ran on the front of their Styles section. Within days, I received a call from the head of acquisitions at Sterling, the publishing arm of bookseller Barnes & Noble. "I love your topic. Can you turn it into a book? Because if you can, we'd like it to be our lead release for new-year's-resolution time in January 2009," he told me. I took on the challenge of writing the book in what they told me would be record time, but not without a lot of fear and uncertainty.

To write a 256-page, heavily footnoted book that would be the first evidence-based book on the science of goal accomplishment and happiness, I had to take steps that put me at risk. Amidst the Great Recession, I closed my coaching practice for four months—which was all the time I had to write the book if I was going to make the deadline. To write productively and without spending too much money, I also moved away from my home for two weeks at a time—returning only to touch base and regroup, and then leave again. It was especially hard because my children were eighteen, fifteen, and twelve at the time, and I had to rely on a network of other moms to take over my daily jobs of cooking, driving, and being an onsite presence for my children after school. I was also covered in hives at one point and had to visit the hospital several times for migraines so severe I couldn't stop vomiting for hours. But in spite of those challenges, I made the deadline. After I'd sent the bulk of writing to my editor, I drove over the Bay Bridge that links the Delaware shores to my home state of Maryland and called my agent to tell him what I'd done. "Ivor, I did it!" I exclaimed, with no small amount of wonderment and awe in my voice.

Several important things happened to me as a result of my taking those financial and emotional risks—because I honestly didn't know if I was capable of writing the book in such a short period of time. The first was that I redefined who I was to myself, much in the same way Kerri Strug says her Olympic vault in 1996 redefined her.[2] I realized that I'd done something challenging under tremendous physical, emotional, and financial pressure, and that in spite of those challenges, I'd written a pioneering book, *Creating Your Best Life,* a book that added something new to the goal-setting and positive-psychology literature. The second important result was revealed to me when I let my clients know that I'd finished the book and was ready to resume coaching—that is, if they still wanted to work with me. I knew when I closed my referral-only practice that many other excellent coaches could happily step into my shoes. To my great surprise, however, I didn't lose a single client. In fact, my practice bulged with old and new clients, which helped to replenish the coffers that were drained when I took the risk of writing the book.

I was so curious about this unexpected outcome that I asked a client about it one day when we reconnected. "Why didn't you hire someone else?" I asked her.

Her response surprised me: "You did something I've never seen anyone else do in real time before, and I wanted to know how it would turn out," she explained. "Everyone always talks about taking risks, following your passions, and not playing it safe, but you're the first person in my life who has ever had the courage to follow her dream despite putting so many things at risk, including the possibility of failing."

I pondered my client's statement for a long time and realized that she was right in her assessment of how often people are encouraged to follow their passion, be courageous, and let the chips fall where they may, yet how few people ever actually do just that. Gary Latham, the cofounder of the goal-setting theory we studied earlier in this book, explained this dynamic to me in an interview I had with him for the book I'd risked so much to write. He said that his research showed that the reason people don't take risks and try to achieve hard goals is they don't want to disappoint themselves. "After all, if you don't shoot for the stars, you can't feel bad about not getting there," he said with a chuckle. "No one wants to feel bad about themselves," he concluded, "and that's why most people at the end of their lives have a 'coulda, shoulda, woulda attitude' about what they haven't accomplished."[3]

Loss-aversion theory also explains the reluctance to let go of something you have, from losing a stock, to an unsatisfying marriage. It's that "losing hurts more than winning feels good," according to the economists who have studied this phenomenon in human behavior. Once we have owned something, even temporarily, we tend to believe it is more valuable than it really is, so when we have to let go of it, it's harder and more upsetting than it ought to be. That's also why we will continue to throw good money after bad, whether we're at a poker table or running a company. People with authentic grit have the ability to be clear-eyed and rational in situations like these, and can cut their losses to salvage a situation and not lose all of their progress.

Did you fail today? High five!

When we decide to take a risk, we are taking a stand about who we want to be. Ruth Chang, a philosophy professor at Rutgers University, said in a TED talk that not making these types of decisions leaves us as "drifters" who never really choose where we want to put our agency. The opportunity to take a risk, though, is a "godsend," she says. "You might say that we become the authors of our lives."[4]

One powerful way to help you take a risk in the right direction is to learn about the failures of other people who also succeed. Sara Blakely, the billionaire founder of Spanx, uses this approach by celebrating the "Oops!" moments her employees have. She also freely shares her own personal and professional mistakes so that her employees learn that people overcome missteps and emerge intact. She credits her open-minded approach to failure to her father, who regularly asked his children at dinner to share their daily failures and responded to them with a high five for their taking chances. He also taught Sara to extract the nuggets of gold from every setback, which left her with the conviction that there are no bad experiences in life, but rather that everything is a teachable moment making you smarter and better prepared for whatever happens. Like many other gritty people, Sara believes that the only failures in life are the failures to take action.[5]

Another CEO, Jim Donald of the national hotel chain Extended Stay America, decided to encourage his employees to take more risks in an innovative way. When the company emerged from bankruptcy, Donald found that many of them were worried about losing their jobs, causing them to avoid making risky decisions that might be costly for the company, such as offering unhappy guests a complimentary night's stay. This risk-averse behavior was preventing the company from coming up with creative solutions to problems or innovating in a pinch, so Donald did something unusual. He created small bright-green cards that said "Get out of jail free," and he distributed them to all nine thousand employees. Whenever they wanted to make a risky decision, all they had to do was use the card and call it in to management.[6]

EXERCISE   A few ways to begin taking more risks

- **Ask yourself "Why not?" instead of "Why?"** Gritty
  people don't stare endlessly at their options, weighing and
  measuring the pros and cons of taking action. They aren't
  impulsive, but they also aren't caught up in making perfect
  decisions or compelled to learn as much as possible before
  moving ahead. I have found that some of my clients who
  are high in the VIA strengths of curiosity, love of learning,
  and critical thinking are the ones who are prone to getting
  stuck in their heads, overthinking and overanalyzing
  whether they should take a risk. Steven Levitt, economist
  and coauthor of *Freakonomics,* found that when people
  hesitate about uprooting themselves and making a major

change, they probably should just do it. He found in twenty thousand cases that when people decide to make a big change—either on their own or as a result of a coin toss—they always are happier because of that change.[7]

- **Start with small risks.** Some of my clients are very successful men and women, but they admit that they don't have enough grit because they have always played it safe, pursuing accomplishments that looked difficult to others but that were actually low-hanging fruit for them. If you are accustomed to being a "winner" because you always stay in your wheelhouse, start taking manageable risks to get comfortable with the emotions of fear, anxiety, and exhilaration. Cut your hair, and try a brand-new look. If you usually overthink all of your purchases, don't research for so long and make a "good enough" decision. Some corporate coaches help clients learn how to do this by giving them physical challenges, such as going down a difficult ski slope with bungee cords attached so they won't hurt themselves, or participating in a ropes course. The idea is that if you can take physical risks, you will take emotional risks more easily.

- **Don't share your goals with negative people.** UCLA researcher Shelly Gable has found that sharing our dreams or early progress toward our goals with people who respond negatively—rather than with the positive responses of curiosity and enthusiasm—can make us abandon our goals, particularly if they are the first people we talk to.[8] Dara Torres, who won a silver medal in the 2008 Olympics in the 50-meter freestyle at the age of 41, was so intent on becoming the oldest swimmer to ever win a medal in the Olympics that in the year leading up to the games, she refused to allow anyone in her presence who did not believe she could be successful.[9] ■

EXERCISE   The payoffs of "failure"

Although it's easy to encourage people to take risks and be prepared for the wonders of failure, it's quite another to actually do so yourself. In this writing exercise, explore some of the failures and setbacks that have occurred in your life and include a recognition of the positives that emerged from these failures—such as the lessons learned, new relationships forged, self-respect enhanced, or lack of regret. Doing this exercise regularly, even as part of a daily reflection, can embolden you to remember that we always find ways to pick ourselves up and live to see another day, and that failing to take any risks at all is the biggest failure we could ever have. ■

13

Humility

Several years ago, a successful entrepreneur—I'll call him Michael—hired me to help him. Michael had hit it big in his twenties, coming up with a financial-organizational system that he sold to major corporations for tens of millions of dollars. His windfall allowed him to take a few years off, and he spent that time circling the globe, investing in real estate, and doing whatever struck his fancy. He later settled down, had a few children, and then devoted himself to building another company as he entered his thirties. He was stuck, though, and wanted to see if a coach could help him understand why he wasn't making headway attracting the right people to join his new venture.

It wasn't long before I began to notice a pattern that helped explain his problem. During our calls, Michael went on about what he'd done that week, told me how confident he was about his ideas for the future, and stressed how successful he'd already been. But when I asked him for his specific goals for our coaching calls, he was often unprepared, and he rarely asked me for feedback. Instead he rattled on, seemingly unaware of his self-absorption. Finally, I asked Michael if he usually monopolized conversations when he met with others and if he ever let others speak or even asked for their opinions. My question brought him up short, but he clearly heard me because the following week Michael thanked me for being so honest. He said he asked his wife what she thought of my question: she was relieved that someone had clued him in.

Michael had been so successful at such an early age that he'd moved into a financial stratosphere most people couldn't comprehend. The people around him often didn't know what to talk to him about, other than to ask him for financial or business advice. Consequently, Michael often droned on for long periods, without being interrupted, and became accustomed to holding court wherever he was. He was rarely challenged, whether or not people agreed with him, because the conversations often turned toward men and women asking if he'd help them in some way with their charity, investment, or other business dealing.

It was a heady place for a young man to be in, and he'd gradually lost his curiosity in others, considering himself the smartest man in the room because that was how most people treated him. Unfortunately, Michael's arrogance was the first thing people probably noticed now. We talked about how new acquaintances, especially those with whom he wanted to collaborate, must feel when he hogged the conversation and rarely let them have airtime. It became clear to Michael that part of his current dilemma about how to move forward was that he hadn't allowed himself to hear new thinking by letting others share their experiences about anything. And he wasn't making a good impression on potential employees.

To his credit, Michael changed. After our deeply personal conversations about how this had come to be his norm and his sobering self-assessment, Michael decided to talk less and listen more, and his conversations with everyone, not just me, became more enjoyable. It was no surprise to me that as he stepped back, making room for reciprocal dialogues and letting others shine, his vision for his new company became clearer. He began to attract the right people, who genuinely liked him and wanted to work with him, and he launched his company a year later. Michael learned that there is more harmony in a team—in fact, in all of his personal relationships as well—when instead of assuming he knows the right answers, he solicits input to help him make better decisions.

Good to great

The ending of Michael's story won't come as a surprise to anyone who has studied leadership or success. When Jim Collins, the author of *Good to Great,* studied the differences between companies that were good and those that had transitioned from good to great, he found that the most exceptional companies are the ones led by CEOs who are high in humility. They built organizations with senior leadership teams that were valued and given the latitude to succeed, and these humble CEOs didn't need to take all the credit. They were also open to feedback and quick to change when problems required it, and their companies were built to last—they didn't collapse when the CEO left.[1]

E. B. White's popular children's book *Charlotte's Web* has a memorable scene in which Charlotte the spider spells the word "humble" in her web to describe Wilbur the pig. When Templeton the rat asks what it means, Charlotte answers, "Not proud," which turns out to be only part of the right answer. A deeper look at the ingredients of humility has found that we see it in two ways: socially and intellectually. Social humility has honesty, thoughtfulness, maturity, and unselfishness at its core, while intellectual humility is made up of curiosity, a willingness to learn from others, and an openness to new ideas. Together, social and intellectual humility define humility as it shows up in studies of character strengths.[2]

When assessing high company performance in individual and team settings, a study from the University of Washington Foster School of Business reinforced the importance of humility as the critical ingredient—Collins calls it the X-factor. It meant that there was a willingness to listen to others, to admit one's own shortcomings in order to learn how to be more effective in the future, and to be confident without conceit. Humility could be one of the key advantages to business success.[3] The same study found that leaders high in humility had staff who were more engaged in their work, more committed to their leader's vision, and more trusting and open to their leader's ideas.

Dean of Harvard Business School Nitin Nohria echoes what his school's research has shown on the importance of humility in leaders. Although leaders can possess a variety of approaches to solving problems and have different outlooks on life, he says that all great leaders possess one key determining trait: reflectiveness.[4] The ability to be thoughtful, take in critical feedback, be honest with oneself and others, and go past superficial analyses is what gives them the clarity and wisdom to take decisive actions with confidence. In so doing, they also gain the respect of others, while role modeling effective leadership, particularly in troubled times.

Research bears out another reason humility is so important to success in settings where the stakes are high and the goals are big. People build bonds with each other when they don't feel they will be exploited, making cooperation more likely. Humility, which has been called the "social oil" that makes this possible, reduces the chances of egotistical, selfish behavior.[5] This isn't just true in professional organizations; it's also true in athletics and in marriages. Take the bestseller *The Boys in the Boat,* which details how the 1936 United States men's rowing team had to work together as a cohesive unit in order to upset the favored Germans. In fact, rowing is often called "the ultimate team sport" because no one person can outshine the others in the boat; it's the collective effort and shared vision of many people working in harmony that crosses the finish line, not the work of any one individual.

Although it may seem counterintuitive, having humility requires courage, because people who are humble are open to self-improvement and are willing to seek out feedback to become better. In fact, a Google survey of their best managers showed that the ones at the top were the ones who asked for critical feedback and then acted upon it.[6] The same is true among many elite athletes, who have also been found to be among the humblest competitors. They never assume that they are guaranteed a win, and will risk failure so they can learn from it and get better. Dr. Wade Rowatt, an associate professor of psychology at Baylor University who studies humility, says that when athletes respect their opponents and conduct themselves with dignity during games, they are the ones who are always better prepared. They are also the ones who have the best reputation after they retire because of their modesty.[7]

How can anyone say they are self-made?

People with humility are grateful for the assistance they get and do not forget who has helped them along the way. Junior Bernard grew up one of nine children in Haiti and recalls that everyone was so poor and hungry in his town that "even the dogs were skinny." His father repaired VCRs for a living, which is how Junior saw clips of American movies, in which he told me that he "always saw people doing exciting things, like going to their job or getting married." He began to dream of moving to the United States to get an education and create a better life. When he found an English dictionary in a trashcan, he used it to begin learning English. He also followed tourists around in the hopes that they would talk to him so he could get better at the language.

Neighbors and the other kids belittled Junior for his dream of escaping the cycle of poverty, and his path was littered with crushing disappointments. His best friend, who had also hoped to leave Haiti for the United States, succumbed to alcohol and drug addiction. Another longstanding family friend stole the money Junior had saved to register for his final year in high school, causing him to drop out and despair that he'd ever find a way to get to the country he dreamed about.

Then Junior met a man, Billy Barr, who'd come to Haiti to volunteer with the Haitian Health Foundation, when he was assigned to be an interpreter for four days. Barr noticed that Junior showed up every day in the blazing sun with freshly pressed clothing, not just interpreting, but also working tirelessly alongside the volunteers until his clothes stuck to his body—never complaining or asking for special favors, the way many of the young Haitians did.

One day, Barr offered Junior his baseball hat to shield his head, but Junior declined, saying that his job's restrictions prevented him from taking anything from anyone. Fascinated, Barr asked the nuns associated with the charity more questions about Junior. When they shared his dream of going to the United States to get an education, Barr wrote the following words to his wife about the possibility of their family helping him: "[I]t would be a shame to have someone that is so intelligent mired in poverty because of a lack of funds." Not long after that, an elated Junior joined the Barr family in New Jersey; despite overwhelming odds against him, he passed the GED exam six months after he arrived, surviving on two hours of sleep a night and sleeping with the GED textbook. Junior went on to win a four-year scholarship to Alvernia University, inspiring everyone he encountered with his story and obvious passion for his newfound country and the chance to make his dreams come true. In 2013, he gave one of the commencement speeches in flawless English, exhorting others to dream big dreams and follow them with passion.[8]

In our interview, Junior shared an astute observation about humility that I'd never thought of, and that no one had yet mentioned to me—he challenged one of the phrases he'd often heard since moving to the United States. "I don't understand how anyone can say they are self-made," he commented in wonderment. "I couldn't have accomplished anything without so many people doing things for me—feeding me when I had nothing to eat, giving me translation jobs when I wanted to talk to Americans, bringing me to the United States and giving me a home to live in. How can anyone accomplish anything without people helping them? How can you make yourself successful all by yourself?"[9]

How givers wind up at the top

Adam Grant is a legend at the University of Pennsylvania's Wharton School because of his quick rise to tenure (in three years) and his innovative approaches to studying success and creativity. His first book, *Give and Take,* looked at how people who are ardent and frequent "givers" wind up at the top of the success ladder, as opposed to where "takers" and "matchers" end up. Not surprisingly, takers have a predictable focus on promoting themselves and will do almost anything to shine, including taking advantage of others and cutting moral corners. One phrase that describes this behavior is "kiss up, kick down."[10]

Grant's book relays a funny story about how Enron's Ken Lay epitomized takers—and faux grit—with his desire to receive favorable, if false, praise. In 1998, Wall Street analysts visited Enron to see how the company was generating profits. To impress them, Lay created a fake scene on a borrowed floor of the building, where employees brought family photos to their pretend desks and made pretend phone calls in which they bought and sold energy as the analysts passed through the scene.

Givers, on the other hand, are humble, which is how they often succeed at their gritty goals. Grant describes givers as people who look for opportunities to meet other people and find out what they need, and who then do whatever they can to be of service. They do this without strings attached, and they do it because they believe everyone ought to have every advantage to succeed. Givers find that making a difference in someone else's life is its own reward, and that when they help others, it results not only in goodwill, but also in their being popular and having a positive reputation, all of which allow givers to amass the support they need when it's time for them to get something done.

Research supports the idea that arrogant people—typically the takers—are less likely than givers to lend a helping hand. Psychologist George Fieldman speculates about these findings, noting that humble people are more in touch with their deficiencies and are empathetic toward others because they respect the boundaries of their own limitations: "Appreciating one's own limits may enable people to empathize with the needs of others and so facilitate altruistic behaviors," he says. "This, in turn, may have other benefits as it may foster acts of reciprocal altruism—so benefiting the altruist and society by default."[11]

Humility run amok

Although it may be hard to believe, the overuse of humility can be as detrimental to success as its underuse. I've coached several CEOs who had humility among their top five character strengths, but instead of using it appropriately, they undersold themselves and were even pushed around by their senior leadership team and employees. One such CEO, whom I'll call Ken, was young and socially awkward. He'd become the head of a new company because of his technological savvy, but had also been raised to defer to authority—in this case, a cadre of older professionals who'd been placed in top positions by the venture capitalists who had funded the company's launch. This background, along with Ken's top five strengths—which included humility, teamwork, and fairness—created the perfect storm for him to become a doormat to be stomped on and a pincushion for incessant needling.

As I sat through my first senior leadership meeting, I was astonished to see open displays of disrespect, contempt, and eye rolling whenever his team disagreed with what Ken was saying. Instead of allowing him to finish his sentences, they'd interrupt him and talk over him. No wonder he had asked me to coach him on becoming more "leaderly"! Ken's tendency to give credit to everyone but himself, to consult others frequently while making decisions in the interest of "teamwork," and to give his leadership team higher salaries than he took himself—so that it wouldn't look "unfair"—left him looking not fair but instead weak, indecisive, and unproductive.

After I coached Ken on how the overuse of his top strengths was actually causing him to be unhappier and less successful, he began to take better control of his relationships with his management team, drawing better boundaries that fostered more respect. As I coached him and also worked with every member of his team, their harmony improved drastically. The meetings became more productive and engaging, and the team even began to behave like friendly colleagues. Teamwork was noticeably more positive, and the company's profits soared.

Although I've seen a number of male leaders misuse humility, it's a more common problem among women leaders, even those for whom humility is not a top-five strength. A study published in the *Academy of Management Journal* reported the findings that leaders who admit mistakes, spot and celebrate followers' strengths, and model "teachability" are predictive of their own and their organization's growth. These leaders, the study says, "model how to be effectively human rather than superhuman, and they legitimize 'becoming' rather than 'pretending.'" *There is a catch, though:* humble leadership tends to benefit white men more than leaders who are young, nonwhite, or female—who instead report that they are constantly called upon to demonstrate their competence. Also, women are expected to show more humility than their male counterparts, which then calls their effectiveness into question. "Our results suggest that female leaders often experience a double bind," one of the researchers, Bradley Owens notes. "They are expected to be strong leaders and humble females at the same time."[12]

The value of humility presents still another conundrum. In Scandinavian countries, which have always ranked among the happiest in the world and which have the highest standards of living, an ingrained aversion to takers and to selfie grit prevails because of a cultural concept known as the Law of Jante. About eighty years ago, this notion of eschewing self-promotion and individual grandiosity arose from Danish novelist Aksel Sandemose's description of the community he knew in childhood, where personal growth was governed by the benefits it would bring to everyone. The Law of Jante consists of ten principles that can be summarized by the statement "You are not to think you are better than us." Today, the Law of Jante is seen by many Danes as a positive hedge against economic risk-taking and overconfident behavior, but many Scandinavians have also come to view it as a barrier to creativity and industriousness.[13]

While humility clearly has benefits, the Law of Jante and others like it, such as the tall-poppy syndrome—a term coined in Australia that describes the need to cut down to size anyone who stands out among others—show the dark side of enforced humility and how it can stifle excellence. Danish leaders are increasingly speaking out against the longstanding Law of Jante and its societal fallout. As prominent Danish commentator Niels Lillelund put it, "In Denmark we do not raise the inventive, the hardworking, the ones with initiative, the successful, or the outstanding; we create hopelessness, helplessness, and the sacred ordinary mediocrity."[14]

One recent example in the United States of the spread of enforced humility that does nothing to promote hard work and excellence is the decision by some high schools to prohibit graduates from wearing designations of exceptional achievement so that all graduates will feel the same, which I discussed earlier. For example, in June

2016, Plano Senior High School in Plano, Texas, a wealthy suburb of Dallas, ruled that graduating seniors couldn't wear the distinctive regalia of the National Honor Society because recognizing their high grades and community service would make them look "special."[15] Going one step further are the many schools I noted that are either eliminating valedictorian status or making it something that dozens of students in each class are granted. One school board in North Carolina has approved removing letter grades from students' report cards and replacing them with Latin designations like cum laude, because, as the board says, "competition is unhealthy."[16] It's hard to see how creating a society of false humility and non-recognition will result in positive outcomes, particularly if excellence is a goal. Without excellence, how can anyone learn how to do anything that is hard or that requires grit?

And there's another type of humility that doesn't ring true: faux humility, also known as "humblebragging." I chuckle daily when I look at examples of this on Facebook, where statements about one's good fortune ("Please pray for me as I go on the *Today* show because I have no idea why they chose my book as a guide to stress in the workplace!") are mixed in with sneaky parental announcements about a child's accomplishments ("Bubba wasn't supposed to be a lifeguard today but he happened to save a child's life while eating lunch at the pool!").

Authentic humility

In the children's story *Goldilocks and the Three Bears,* Goldilocks enters the house and progressively eats the porridge, sits in the chairs, and sleeps in the beds of the three bears, proclaiming "Just right!" when she eats the third bear's porridge, sits in his chair, and sleeps in his bed. As I mull over the research on humility, its overuse and underuse and its role in cultivating authentic grit, I see that it requires getting humility just right in order to experience its full benefits.

Humility for the right reason and in the right dose is authentic humility, and when it is imbued with curiosity, generosity, vulnerability, an openness to critical feedback, and a willingness to grow, humility gives fuel to the fire of grit. With this kind of humility, you respect the challenges ahead of you and prepare with guidance from others. You grow your team of support through unselfish behavior and a desire to see others shine, too. Your setbacks aren't met with petulance but instead with an understanding of your limitations and a desire to become better. You are not afraid to stand out, but you also don't seek the limelight to prop up your ego. And finally, you understand the gravity of being a role model, yet you wear the crown lightly.

EXERCISE   Ways to cultivate humility

- **If you are prone to taking a lot of selfie photos and posting them on social media, take a break for a week or longer and carefully assess how you feel.** Research has found that people who frequently post selfies and updates about themselves score lower on measures of belonging and meaningfulness, and can feel like their self-esteem rises and falls based on likes.[17] If you must be on social media, post pictures of pets, friends, and scenery, which has been found to make people more likeable.

- **Set a goal to not talk about yourself for at least one day, and instead be curious about other people and their goals.** Encourage them to tell you what they most need to be successful, and see if you can help them. In other words, become one of the "givers" Adam Grant describes in *Give and Take.*

- **Seek critical feedback from someone who is better than you at something you are trying to accomplish.** Don't ask someone who is just going to try to please you and stroke your ego. Get specific points that will help you improve your skills and behavior in meaningful ways.

- **Write a real thank-you note (or email if it means you will definitely do it) to someone who has helped you achieve an important goal.** The essence of humility is to know who has been instrumental in your growth and acknowledge those people appropriately. One of the upsides to expressing gratitude is that it also improves well-being, which is the precursor to all success. ■

EXERCISE   **Toot someone else's horn**

One of the nicest strengths about authentically gritty people is that they build bridges to other people by being supportive and generous. One of the ways to become humble enough to tout someone else's wins is to find out what they've accomplished and how they did it, and then share it with others. When we can be excited and curious about other people's good news, it's called "active constructive responding," and when we share their good news and encourage them to replay their success, we help others to "capitalize," which further builds well-being. So learn how to do this if it's not yet in your skill set.

Interview someone about what they view as one of their greatest accomplishments. Take the time to find out why it was meaningful to them, which strengths they used, and what has happened as the result of that accomplishment. Use curiosity to delve as deeply as possible by asking "what" and "how" questions. Then share that person's story with someone else, and take note of how it feels to see someone else shine in other people's eyes with you as the messenger. Is it hard for you to share the spotlight? Why or why not? Do you feel a sense of well-being when you promote someone else? What else do you feel? ■

14

Perseverance

he Tong Leong School of Martial Arts is the last martial-arts academy many would expect to find in the privileged community of Bethesda, Maryland, where most youngsters are accustomed to easy lives of high-quality schools, first-class sports opportunities, and bright futures. Unlike the pervasive "McDojos" that serve up black belts once you've paid a certain amount of money or spent a specific number of months at different ranks, at the Tong Leong School you earn what is around your waist with years of hard work and no set timeline. And that is on purpose.

The founder and head of the school, Paul Thomas, a ninth-degree black belt in Tzee Wai Kuen and Tong Leong, has been practicing the martial arts for thirty-five years, starting as a youth, when he lived in the rough and tumble Dunlap and Delaney Apartments in the projects of Perth Amboy, New Jersey. Abandoned by his biological father, but happily secure in his tight family of his mother and stepfather, Thomas is a classic study in the rewards of gritty perseverance.

Taking on a paper route before school at age eleven, Thomas doesn't know what it's like not to work hard—and he only quits when the job is done. Although he had to beg his mother to let him take on various jobs throughout his teens—from working in a movie theater, to setting up banquets at the Sheraton Hotel, to working as a waiter at Red Lobster, to cleaning parking lots—Thomas never let his grades slip and was a popular three-sport star athlete right through high school graduation.

His parents, who also worked several jobs during the day and at night (his stepfather, Climmie, as a maintenance man in the projects, and his mother, Sandra, in a variety of jobs including accounts receivable and community activism), were role models of fortitude and no whining. When they began to clean nearby office buildings at night for extra money, Thomas insisted on helping out. When his parents dropped him off at one building as they went to another, he was intent on seeing how quickly he could get his portion of the work done so that they could all end as soon as possible.

When Thomas was twenty-one and learned from his girlfriend, Tanita, that she was pregnant, he worked even harder so that his parents wouldn't have to pay for his new responsibilities. Although money was tight and the odds of them making it were slim, Thomas and Tanita moved into their own apartment. He got a good job in the prison system, worked as many shifts as possible, and saved every penny so that the couple could stand on their own and give their baby daughter, Quanisha, a stable life.

Thomas gradually built his reputation not just as a disciplined worker at whatever he set out to do, but also as a model of fitness, winning a national body-building contest, The Naturals, in which no steroids or other performance-enhancing drugs are permitted. Eventually, he moved into training other people full-time and was then recruited by the Congressional Country Club in Bethesda, home to golf's US Open and the playground of numerous presidents, celebrities, and powerful business leaders. There, Thomas created a boot camp that is the most popular offering in their fitness center.

Although it would be easy to settle in to the security and distinction he has earned and simply continue as he is now, Thomas has begun to focus on passing along the life lessons he has gotten from the martial arts, partly because they gave him such a good base and partly because the area where he lives is in real need of the same values he believes create the perseverance and grit that have brought him so many positive results.

Today, four men and one woman are sweating their way through a two-and-a-half-hour training session in which Thomas enforces discipline and repetition of the fundamentals. "Get the stance right; that's your base, C.J. Toes out, Demetrius. Do it again," he says. "Yes, sir," is the response, hundreds of times, followed by a respectful bow. Later,

Thomas explains to me that as rigorous as his school is, the real goal is to teach people how to be a martial artist in all parts of their lives.

"It takes you to another level of discipline, focus, and persistence," he explains, "and that's what I used to get me out of the projects and to achieve my goals. The martial arts humble you and teach you that while you might be a higher belt, someone with a lower belt can be better than you at something, and you can learn from them. You are never finished here—just like in life, you can't just give up because something is hard."

Thomas's secret to success is exactly what the research has found to be effective when it comes to being persistent when you have a big goal. His goal was to get out of the projects and out of Perth Amboy, a goal he set when he was young and his mother drove him to see the big homes in Asbury Park. "I saw the gleam in her eye, and I knew she was dreaming as much for me as she was for herself," he remembers. "She made sure I saw things that lit me up and made me aware of what I could strive for. She took me to see the ocean in North Carolina. No one in the projects saw the ocean! She was friends with people from all walks of life and of all colors. She showed me that you can build relationships with anyone, regardless of your background. Through her, I learned to work hard and not to quit, and she made sure I was surrounded by people in sports and the martial arts who gave me the tools to become a man who could carry himself with dignity and humility."[1]

"Struggling well"

Why people like Paul Thomas can find ways to thrive and work hard toward personal achievements, regardless of being born without the advantages of kids, say, in Bethesda, is a question that has been studied for hundreds of years by philosophers, psychologists, and motivational speakers. In 1907, psychologist William James called upon his peers to find out why some people were able to dig deeper than others to succeed while others simply languished without tapping into their potential strengths. James wrote to his peers in *Science* magazine, "The human individual lives usually far within his limits; he possesses powers of various sorts which he habitually fails to use. He energizes below his maximum, and he behaves below his optimum . . . the habit of inferiority to our full self—that is bad."[2]

Positive psychology's Chris Peterson was fond of saying that thriving people are good at "struggling well."[3] As we all know, life is full of challenges, particularly if we choose to set grand goals, but what separates people who don't have grit from people who do is often this issue of working hard and overcoming difficulties without losing focus, equanimity, or passion—that is, struggling well. So, if you want to cultivate grit but you don't have a constructive relationship with discomfort, failure, and delayed gratification, it's imperative to find ways to make your peace with these conditions.

One of the most intriguing findings in Angela Duckworth's research on grit is that high-grit people hate hard work as much as those who don't have high grit. High-grit people simply accept hard work as the price they must pay to get where they want to go, and so they find ways to do it. As the late boxer and humanitarian Muhammad Ali put it, "I hated every minute of training but I said, 'Don't quit. Suffer now and live the rest of your life as a champion.'" Duckworth's research on the finalists in the National Spelling Bee found that the boys and girls who advanced the furthest in the Bee were not the ones who played word games on the computer or who were quizzed by their parents, but the ones who spent time in solitary study of words and their etymology. These high-achieving children simply accepted that mastery of words meant there were going to be occasions where they had no choice except to isolate themselves with study guides and log the necessary hours without distraction.

Bob Bowman, the only swim coach Michael Phelps has had, is fond of saying that there are no secrets to Michael Phelps's legendary greatness. He notes that Phelps never missed a workout at the pool between the ages of twelve and eighteen, building the foundation of "everyday excellence" without any shortcuts.[4] And with a nod to the absence of "selfie grit" in Phelps and other champions who show up at cold pools for punishing workouts morning, noon, and night, Under Armour aired a line of commercials leading up to the 2016 Rio

Olympics—Phelps's last—with the tagline "It's what you do in the dark that shows up in the light."[5]

Procrastination and the many ways "to skin a cat"

One of the things gritty people do as they work toward their goals is learn how to overcome procrastination, a problem that has gotten worse in recent decades because of technology and the many ways it distracts us. Defined as "the voluntary delay of an action despite foreseeable negative future consequences," procrastination has been studied by researchers to understand how it happens and what can be done to combat it.[6]

One of the simplest techniques for overcoming this obstacle that works for many is adopting the mind-set that any delay will not even be considered. I remember first reading about this approach years ago in an interview with an accomplished yoga teacher who was asked how she'd been able to create and sustain a daily practice for many years, regardless of what was going on in her life. "I don't allow the idea of not practicing to cross my mind," she answered.

"Implementation intentions" are also a helpful strategy to combat procrastination. First put forth by researcher Peter Gollwitzer, implementation intentions are also known as if-then conditions, which are the use of environmental cues to trigger positive actions.[7] For example, "When it is five o'clock, I will walk the puppy," or "When I put on my running shoes, I will leave the house within five minutes." These if-then conditions make it more likely you will follow through on your goals because you have made an agreement with yourself ahead of time. "Behavioral contracts" like these succeed because they conserve mental energy that might otherwise be used by "Will I or won't I?" ideas, which open the door to procrastinating or not doing what you intended to do. I suspect the yoga teacher I read about had a version of an "if-then" agreement with herself, something like, "If I start to wonder whether I will practice, I won't entertain the thought any further."

Professor Timothy Pychyl of Carleton University has studied and written about procrastination for many years, and he says that giving in to the urge to feel good in the moment is at the heart of procrastination, but the rub is that giving in makes you feel worse later and gets under your skin as a failure of character. For some, doing physical exercise instead of focusing on their work is a temporary relief, called "moral compensation," because they're actually doing something positive—but what they're doing still keeps them from accomplishing the difficult task at hand.[8]

One key reason people procrastinate is what's called "anticipation of a hassle," which means that we expect getting started on a task will take more time and energy than we currently have.[9] The most successful technique for conquering "anticipation of a hassle" is to set a timer and tell yourself that you are going to work on the task for ten minutes. Almost invariably, the ten minutes gets you over the hump and allows you to keep moving in the right direction.

Another way to get started when you feel tempted to put something off is to make it harder for yourself to engage in delaying behaviors— essentially putting something like a cabinet between you and a Pop-Tart, instead of leaving it on the counter in plain view. Writers are so familiar with procrastination, which they often call writer's block, that solutions for it have proliferated for centuries—including Victor Hugo's, which was to lock away his day clothes until he'd finished his daily writing quota.[10]

Another suggestion from Pychyl, Piers Steel, and Alexander Rozental, who have all studied this topic, is to look into the future and vividly imagine yourself having completed the goal, focusing on all the positive emotions you will feel once you finish. This approach is effective because procrastinators tend to have "temporal myopia"—that is, they are often unable to plan how to accomplish long-term goals effectively, so putting them in touch with the future and all of its hoped-for positive emotions overrides any impulsive decision to procrastinate.[11] Combining incremental visual goals with small internal celebrations is a variation that Maria Parker, one of the finest long-distance cyclists in the United States, uses to persevere and keep herself going for hours and hours. "I just make tiny goals for myself," she told me, "like I tell myself that I'm going to get to the crack in the sidewalk on the next street, and then when I get there, I say, 'Yay!' or, 'Yippee! You go, girl!'"[12]

The power of words:
what we say and what we hear

Researchers in the field of psycholinguistics study the effect words have on our attitudes and behaviors. A study from this field showed that the name of a game alone had a powerful impact, as people who played a game called the Wall Street Game were less cooperative than those playing the game called Community Game.[13] Sports-psychology research has found that the moment the brain allows phrases like "I'm done" or "I can't go any farther" to take hold, the body follows, because it won't quit until the brain tells it to.[14]

The words used in slogans at twelve-step meetings are often credited with helping alcoholics and other addicts persist in their daily fight to abstain for another twenty-four-hour period. Sayings such as "One day at a time," "Attitude of gratitude," and "Easy does it" are known to legions of twelve-step members, who say the short phrases are easy to remember and implement when they're tempted to go astray. Many people cite biblical and other spiritual phrases as their touchstone for emotional resilience. Some of the phrases I heard most often in my interviews with paragons of grit were "Yea, though I walk through the valley of the shadow of death, I shall fear no evil" (Psalm 23); "Blessed is the one who perseveres under trial" (James 1:12); and "Forgetting what is behind and straining toward what is ahead, I press on toward the goal to win the prize" (Philippians 3:13–14).

I once read a very moving story about a pro basketball player who lost his fiancée to suicide and then withdrew from his sport and other people for months. He feared he would never regain his enthusiasm for life, but after studying the Bible for guidance, he realized one day that most of the encouraging stories included the phrase, "Get up!" Once he realized that, depression's hold on him was broken, and he "got up" and got back to the world of the living.[15] As his story illustrates, people find the phrases that speak in unique ways to them, and possibly not to anyone else in the same way, so it's important to make sure that you tune in to your own "channel" of grit, and not anyone else's.

Remember Carol Dweck and her research on children and the fixed mind-set versus the growth mind-set that we looked at earlier in this book, and how the growth mind-set is most common among gritty people? Dweck has gone one step further in her research and discovered that the use of the simple word "yet" can create greater persistence when facing challenges. If you tell a child that they "didn't answer the math questions correctly *yet*," that one word opens their minds to the idea that they can eventually solve the problems. She found that not only did the children become grittier, they also became more zestful, creative, and hopeful when "yet" opened up their eyes to the possibility of a different, limitless future. If "yet" can change mind-set, imagine how many other words and phrases can unlock resilience and stick-to-itiveness!

And just as positive words have the power to shape positive outcomes, allowing negative talk to fill your mind can undo your best efforts before you even get started. I was listening to golf great Jack Nicklaus one day as he talked about his experiences with golfers when they had to play in challenging weather conditions. He found that how people talked about the weather ended up predicting how they did that day. "I'd mentally check people off the list if I heard them complaining," he said, "and I'd say to myself, 'Well, they are done for the day.'"[16]

One of my clients, the top salesman at a car dealership, told me that whenever he saw people clustered in the lunchroom or around a water cooler, he instinctively knew not to go back there. "They are inevitably complaining when they are grouped together like that, because misery loves company, and I don't want to infect myself with any negative feelings or words because I won't be able to make a sale," he said. He's right: Remember the research I noted earlier that showed how even passing by a conversation filled with negative words can change your mind-set? Clearly, taking control over your mind and what it contains is key to becoming gritty. The good news is that the skills are accessible to anyone who wants them.

Acting "as if"—gladiators, basketball mascots, and combat prep

Few would argue that the American game of football takes grit of all kinds. In this environment, to maximize the chances of staying sharp and fit and determined, the mind-set of players has a big role. One athlete, Josh Norman, made headlines for dealing with this reality in an inventive and fun way. Norman, a star cornerback with the Carolina Panthers (and now with the Washington Redskins), spends many hours in the days leading up to games creating a persona he will enact on the field. He decides which superhero or brave character he will be from a movie, and then studies the songs, scripts, and other materials to soak up as much information as possible.

For example, in one game he pretended to be Russell Crowe's character Maximus from *Gladiator*—he even rode a pretend horse after a good play (he was fined for excessive celebration)—and on another occasion, he pretended to be Achilles from the Trojan War movie *Troy*. Opponents never know who he will be, which keeps them off balance, and meanwhile Norman keeps his zest and passion for football alive by bringing novelty to every game.[17]

Norman's actions are familiar to people who talk themselves into doing hard things by "acting as if." I recall when I was a white belt in the Hapkido martial art, the grandmaster instructed all of us to "walk like black belts" because it would hasten our progress in the program. This same strategy was given to me in my twelve-step program when I was first overcoming my eating disorder. I was told to "bring the body, and the mind would follow" whenever I wasn't sure how to handle a situation, like a wedding, in which the cake would be forced into my hands. By acting "as if" I was in the body of a recovered bulimic, I was promised that my mind would see me as that person, too, with important beneficial outcomes. It worked then, and it has continued to work in other tough situations in which pretending I had the character strength I wanted imbued me with the ability to "fake it" until I made it.

About ten years ago, my husband gave me one of the best presents I've ever received: an opportunity to be Testudo, the turtle mascot, at a University of Maryland basketball game. This wouldn't excite everyone,

I know, but my time in the Testudo suit was exhilarating—and instructive. Because I felt free to do whatever I wanted in the suit, I found myself being as silly, spontaneous, and outrageous as I wanted. I ran up into the audience and patted bald men on their heads and watched everyone around them giggling in response. I joined the cheerleaders in the center court, and while they did their carefully choreographed dances, I kicked and punched and shook my shell with vigor. What if we could all try on the personalities that we long to experience in a way that offers a reasonable risk, without much downside?

This is exactly what the new virtual-reality programs are doing in a variety of arenas to help change people's responses to stimuli, assisting them in optimal ways when they are under stress or need to summon up an action that will help them succeed, regardless of how they feel or what is happening around them. For example, the USC Institute for Creative Technologies has created a program called STRIVE (Stress Resilience in Virtual Environments) that helps soldiers prior to combat deployment. They experience traumatic events within a safe environment and are guided through their emotional responses to stress as they cultivate resilience.[18] One of my dreams for the future is that virtual-reality games will allow us to "try on" behaviors that help us to become grittier, and that by vividly experiencing those scenarios, we'll be able to come back into the real world with more patience, willpower, passion, and determination.

Failing forward with Harry Potter

Gritty people often persevere because of previous failure, which haunts them and drives them forward. This phenomenon is called "the psychology of the near miss," and researchers have found that pursuing a goal and getting close, but not actually achieving that goal, activates the rewards processing system.[19] So, instead of failure discouraging future risk-taking, going after something valuable and not succeeding can actually result in greater persistence toward goals. This would explain why so many entrepreneurs who fail at their first company (or more!) emerge with the smarts and stamina that finally nets them a win. The research gives empirical support to the old saying, "If at first you don't succeed, try, try again!"

J.K. Rowling used the occasion of her now-famous 2008 Harvard Commencement speech to instruct graduates on "the benefits of failure." Just seven years after graduating from university, she had "failed on an epic scale"—a busted marriage and close to homeless with an infant. Like other gritty people who persevere in the face of setbacks, though, she used failure to spur her to finally pursue her true passion, which was writing novels. "I stopped pretending to myself that I was anything other than what I was and began to direct all my energy into finishing the only work that mattered to me. Had I really succeeded at anything else, I might never have found the determination to succeed in the one arena I believed I truly belonged. I was set free, because my greatest fear had been realized . . . and so rock bottom became the solid foundation on which I rebuilt my life."[20]

Early birds and night owls

People with grit take advantage of every opportunity to make themselves productive. It's not just that they overcome procrastination, work hard when they have to, and learn from setbacks; they also learn from previous experience about where and how they do their best work, and come up with ways to make themselves most effective. One way they do this is by not wasting time trying to be successful when their bodies and brains aren't optimized for the activity.

Daniel Kahneman, who won a Nobel Prize in economics for his work in behavioral economics, studied what are called diurnal rhythms to find out how people felt at different times of day and if how they felt was correlated with the actual time of day.[21] He found that although most negative emotions are felt at the start of the day, that is also the time when people feel most competent and energized. People hit their peak emotions around competence and energy at noon, and then these emotions decline for the rest of the day until bedtime. Not unsurprisingly, many high achievers are up early, which has also been noted in studies of CEOs, the vast majority of whom are early birds.[22]

Outstanding violinists reported to K. Anders Ericsson, one of the most prominent researchers of expert performance (and who is credited with the 10,000-Hour Rule), that they do their hardest work in the morning as well, followed by a break. They return to their practice before and after lunch, ending their day of practice with about four-and-a-half hours total of focused work. They restore their energy with naps and other mindful behaviors, including meals, a finding that was echoed in studies of chess players, athletes, scientists, artists, and writers.[23]

Working in small, intense chunks of time isn't just good for maximum effort. Daniel Coyle wrote in his book *The Talent Code* that he connected this approach with the laying down of myelin on neural sheaths, which is how behaviors are learned and ingrained. When we work in smart, decisive, and focused ways to succeed in small, leveraged goals, the neural sheaths will create pathways in the body to make it easier to remember and repeat those actions so that they become automatic habits.

Beware the demon alcohol

Karlyn Pipes, author of *The Do-Over* and an International Hall of Fame swimmer mentioned earlier, told me that whenever she is faced with a challenge, her first mental reaction is always, "No. I'm not going to do that." But ever since she got sober, at the age of thirty-one, she can hear a small voice chime in after the initial "no."

"There's a quiet voice that whispers to me and says, 'You can do this. What are you so afraid of? What are you made of today, Karlyn?' I feel like my brain is cracked when it comes to these challenges, and I have to fuse it together like a broken pot, one piece at a time," she said. "I always get to a 'yes,' but it's little by little, one word at a time, one stroke at a time. When I was drinking, the 'no' would be followed by a drink. But I see myself as a blob of moldable clay now, and if I don't put myself in the fire, I'll never know what I could have become."[24]

Pipes-Neilsen raises an important point about the role of alcohol in perseverance. As noted earlier in this book, Roy Baumeister's research on self-regulation has found that alcohol is the number-one deterrent to achieving goals because it reduces all barriers to self-destructive behavior.[25] On more than one occasion, I've had clients tell me that some of their biggest regrets stem from alcohol and the price they've paid for allowing it to steal their initiative, willpower, and resolve. When they're tackling big goals, many of my clients choose to abstain from alcohol to see if it makes a difference, and it always does. Setting the right goals, developing the right mind-set, and doing all of the prep work to be gritty will be meaningless if you can't say "no" to yourself when you need to.

The Zeigarnik effect

Gritty people work in a way that evokes the Zeigarnik effect, which means that they always have unfinished goals pulling them forward. This theory comes from Bluma Zeigarnik, a researcher who noticed that waiters in a restaurant who were still trying to complete a diner's order could recall the details of that order, while waiters who had successfully finished their work with a table couldn't recall the details of the order they had just delivered. Zeigarnik refined these initial observations through various tests until she finally concluded that those working toward a goal who code it as completed in their minds don't then have a restlessness that drives them to continue working on the goal. People who don't quit at goals, however, always have something whirring in the background of their minds, whether they're trying to figure out how to solve a problem, find the right resources, or search for new ways to succeed.[26]

At one point, I was advised that I would have a much easier time finishing my books if I left my manuscript in the middle of a half-written sentence before returning to work on it again. I had no idea why that would be helpful, but when I learned about the Zeigarnik effect, I realized that this trick productive writers use not only keeps them from having to reassemble their thoughts and data from the previous day, but also prepares them to jump right back in. And what a great tip to help avoid procrastination as well because all barriers to starting are removed!

Why does the Zeigarnik principle work particularly well for people who are passionate about their long-term goals? First, when you have a powerful "why" behind what you are doing and you are intrinsically motivated to do this difficult thing because it is important to you, and not necessarily to anyone else, you will instinctively be pulled back to what is unfinished. The other reason it works so well is because when people expect to do well with their goals—when they have high hope and robust self-efficacy—they continue to come back to create completion. So a sure test of whether or not you are truly motivated to achieve a goal is if you respond to unfinished business with passion, curiosity, and zest. If not, you might not be pursuing a gritty goal that is right for you.

EXERCISE   Ways to cultivate perseverance

- **Embed gritty people in your environment.** Angela Duckworth's research has discovered that grit is a contagious behavior, so find ways to embed all kinds of people with authentic grit in your day-to-day life. The head football coach at Harpeth High School in Tennessee said that having assistant coach Kevin Downs, an Iraq war veteran, around the team changed the character of the high school players. Downs nearly lost his life in the war and endured seventy-six surgeries to cope with his injuries. "We have a lot fewer whiners since he started working here," the head coach said.[27]

- **Do things with people who are pursuing similar goals.** Intriguing research on athletes has found that rowers and runners who train together become faster and stronger than when they do those same actions alone. When we are accountable to other people, we are more likely to follow through, and when the environment is positively contagious and intense, we all benefit—after all, "A rising tide lifts all boats," right? It's even been found that people become more productive when they are just in the presence of other industrious people, which is why so many people congregate at libraries and coffee shops to get work done.

- **Act "as if."** Like Josh Norman of the Washington Redskins, who gets into character for his bruising football games by coming up with a persona that he immerses himself in, try acting "as if" you are a gritty person and do whatever that persevering person would do. Remind yourself to act like someone who embodies the person you want to be—history has given us so many choices that we should have no trouble coming up with a suitable role model and script for whatever tough goal we are trying to achieve. This is the principle behind the popular strategy "What would Jesus do?" or "WWJD?" that some people use when in doubt.

- **Bet on yourself.** Incentives to accomplish big goals, especially financial incentives, have been found to work in a variety of situations, particularly with hard goals.

- **Expose yourself to stories of overcoming.** If you don't live or work in an environment where it's common to hear and celebrate stories of overcoming hardship, cultivating resilience, and learning from failure, create one. Whether for yourself or for your child if you are a parent, look to the family lore of ancestors who had to overcome difficulties, from losing a spouse to suffering a financial setback. If you don't have such family tales, there are still plenty of stories to mine: There are the memoirs and biographies of well-known and not-so-well-known people who have been inspired to share their stories of achievement or triumph over adversity. There are also the stories of people in your everyday life. At the Murphy Middle School in Murphy, Texas, they came up with an ingenious idea for gathering these stories after I gave several talks on the importance of grit. A "Grit Committee" thought up *The Stall Street Journal,* a publication featuring the stories of school administrators and teachers and the setbacks they've overcome in their lives, which were posted in the school's bathrooms. The goal is for students to see examples of authority figures who have survived hard times in their daily environment, which could also give them the confidence to approach those teachers for encouragement and advice, if needed.

- **Create an avatar to experience new possibilities in yourself.** Some of the most interesting and exciting developments in technology revolve around the brain changes that occur when we enter a virtual-reality world where we can watch ourselves do things as an avatar that we cannot do in real life. For example, one study found that an agoraphobe who hadn't left her house in ten years, and whose therapy had failed in helping her do so, created an avatar in a game called *Second Life* who looked like her but who had an extroverted personality and went to lots of parties and other gatherings. The woman identified so strongly with the avatar that she was able to overcome her agoraphobia. (Essentially, this is the same thing you do when you act "as if.") Jeremy Bailenson, director of the Virtual Human Interaction Lab at Stanford University, explains that avatars work because they can trigger genuine emotions and reactions, even in situations or experiences beyond our normal capacities. "There is good reason to believe that our avatars change how we interact with others," he said.[28] Many promising new technologies and immersive realities, including video games, are teaching people to overcome self-limiting fears and to cultivate courage, resilience, teamwork, and perseverance, which play an important role in the development of grit. ▪

EXERCISE   Three hard things

One of the most widely embraced exercises from positive psychology is designed to increase people's feelings of gratitude and happiness by having them count their blessings at the end of the day. "Three Hard Things" is a takeoff on that idea, but this exercise is about listing the three hardest things that were done that day. Research has found that we scan our day at the end of every day for what we did that was hard because those are the things that build our self-confidence and experience of mastery—and when we feel this way about ourselves, we're more likely to persevere toward cherished goals. This is an exercise worth doing regularly, if not nightly.

Write down the three hard things you did today. Explain what made them difficult and how you did them, which includes identifying the strengths you used. ■

15

Patience

One day my phone rang and on the other end was a 29-year-old woman—I'll call her Leanne—standing on the streets of San Francisco, with a business plan for a new company in her purse. She'd heard about my coaching from another Silicon Valley entrepreneur who thought I could be helpful, she said, but she was working on a tight timeline and wanted to know if I was available immediately.

"Everyone out here has a company by the time they turn thirty, and I'm turning thirty in a few months," she told me. "I have an idea for a Web business that I feel certain will be successful, but I keep coming up with reasons not to pursue it. And if I don't do it now, I'll never do it."

After getting more background on Leanne's idea and her motivation for going in this direction, I decided to work with her. She was passionate about the value she knew she could bring to others with her innovative approach, and she knew that if she were accountable to me to take the necessary risks and follow through on her goals, she'd succeed—and, boy, did she. Leanne filed papers to incorporate her business the day before she turned thirty, and within a year was featured on design shows, in entrepreneur magazines, and even on the stage at an international economic summit.

Leanne's impatience to succeed at an age when many young adults in generations past used to wonder what they would be when they grew up isn't uncommon any longer, particularly in a part of the country where people have been known to sell their first company for several million dollars before even getting a college degree. Although a certain amount of impatience can be useful when it comes to setting a deadline about moving forward—like Leanne had with her thirtieth birthday—it can also be hazardous if the person is overly eager to attain the wrong things and lacks the ability to delay gratification in the areas that do matter in gritty goal pursuit. As one Chinese proverb says, "One moment of patience may ward off great disaster. One moment of impatience may ruin a whole life."

"Freaking out" about Einstein

People with authentic grit cultivate the virtue of patience because they don't set short-term goals; their ambitions are long term and are rarely, if ever, achieved in a few months. Take the example of the team of scientists who spent the better part of their careers trying to prove the last portion of Einstein's theory of relativity on the existence of gravitational waves. In September 2015, one hundred years after Einstein's work made its debut, a few scientists discovered that two black holes had collided in space one billion light years away, creating a faint chirp on a machine designed to pick up these very frequencies, the most sensitive scientific instrument ever built.

When the announcement of this stunning breakthrough was broadcast from the California Institute of Technology on February 11, 2016, the leaders who had spearheaded this quest at the Laser Interferometer Gravitational-Wave Observatory were well past traditional retirement age: one man was in his seventies, while the other two were in their eighties, one suffering from dementia.

People who understood the significance were agog. "I think this will be one of the major breakthroughs in physics for a long time," said Szabolcs Marka, a Columbia University professor who was working on the project. Others who heard of the results or read about them in the paper when it was announced alternately described themselves as having "goose bumps" or "freaking out."[1]

Tell that emoji to get me a pizza now!

The idea of devoting one's life to attempting to solve a scientific theory, a road sure to be filled with discouragement, delay, and possible failure, is a hard sell these days when immediate gratification is the norm. Leanne's generation grew up with instantaneous access to all kinds of things, an ease of attainability that make it difficult to know how to wait for anything. If you seek an answer, ask your smartphone. Don't want to stand in line at a restaurant, buy your own coffee, wash your clothes, or even shop for groceries? Apps and services like TaskRabbit and Nowait make it easy to delegate anything that might involve personal discomfort or unnecessary delay. It's even possible to get a pizza delivered to you without using your vocal chords or standing up: just send a text of a pizza emoji to the Domino's Pizza website. Patrick Doyle, the CEO of the company who oversaw the launch of this service, notes, "It's the epitome of convenience . . . we've got this down to a five-second exchange."[2]

The Pew Research Center's Internet & American Life Project has noted that the "hyperconnected" lives of adults under the age of thirty-five comes with significant downsides, reporting that "Negative effects include a need for instant gratification and loss of patience."[3] One study found that tolerance for simply starting up a video had plummeted; after two seconds, people stop waiting, and after thirty seconds, 80 percent of computer users abandon the effort altogether. "Our expectation of 'instant' has become faster," one researcher said, adding that one of his studies had found that those forced to wait for a download who were put on hold at a call center simply hung up rather than wait for service.[4]

The search for immediacy is having an impact on activities that always brought pleasure and rewards but that now feel so effortful that participation is lagging. Quick fun through apps like Candy Crush Saga is trumping the desire to read books. Americans are also saving less money than ever, dropping from 9.7 percent of disposable income being saved in 1982 to 3.6 percent in 2012. "We're not wired to think about the long-term anymore," says Phil Fremont-Smith of ImpulseSave, a company whose app tracks spending and sends congratulatory messages when members cut costs.[5]

The bestselling book on productivity, *The 4-Hour Workweek*, popularized the idea that we should never spend time on anything that isn't our "genius work" and that delegating tasks and unpleasant chores that could be done more easily and economically by others is superior because we'll get more done, get richer, and have more leisure time.[6] This encouragement gave rise to websites like Upwork and Elance, which outsource projects like PowerPoint creation, accounting, writing, and most anything else you can think of, making it easier to accomplish things in the minimum amount of time. In fact, I can't think of an entrepreneur or CEO I have worked with who didn't use these types of services when they were in a pinch and needed immediate help getting a job out the door.

Although I've seen a certain type of impatience be a positive spur to action—as with Leanne and other clients of mine who know that their time is better spent on things they cannot outsource or delegate—our culture now prods us to believe that we should never have to wait for anything or do hard things because someone else can do it for us. If you don't believe me, check out the Yellow Pages, commercials, or business signs in your community. Don't you want to patronize a Qwicky Kleen car detailer, an EZ Loan Center, or a Sir Speedy Copy Service? How can you resist promises like In-N-Out Burger and Three Minute Therapy? Would anything sell with names like Math Made Hard, U Wait Here, or Not Fast Food?

Does anyone long for anything anymore?

I was having lunch in downtown Washington, DC, one afternoon and talking with a colleague about the research on people's current inability to be patient and the fact that the average human attention span is one second less than that of a goldfish (seven seconds and eight seconds, respectively), when she suddenly got a faraway look in her eyes and told me a story that got to the heart of what a difference patience can make in a person's life.

"When I was in second grade, I asked my parents for an expensive doll that I saw at my favorite toy store," she recounted. "They told me that if I saved my money, I could get it before the year was over. So I did as many chores as I could, and I saved my allowance for six months until I finally had earned enough to get that doll. I went to the store with my mother, and I can still remember how excited I was to open my change purse and give the storeowner the money I'd earned all by myself. I was so proud, and I think I loved that doll even more than I would have if my parents had bought it for me when I first asked for it."

As she spoke, I thought about the mistakes I'd made repeatedly with my own children when they were growing up, how I'd often given in to their requests to buy a set of Legos, a snack, or a game, without making them earn their own money or wait until a later date. Some of this had happened because I was lazy and just wanted their whining or fighting to end; other times, I wanted to see them be happy—even though the satisfaction of getting the item didn't last more than a few hours or days. I know that their occasional impatience for a quick fix in later years wasn't just because of proliferating technology and the shortcuts society encourages; it was also because I hadn't sat through the discomfort of seeing them be unhappy when I knew I could make it go away by opening my wallet.

When we teach children to have patience and to wait for what they want, we give them stock that pays valuable dividends for decades. Learning to anticipate a future event—like saving for an iPhone or a trip—has been found to create a sense of optimism and longing that results in more satisfaction with the item when it's acquired. Shoppers even report that they are more dissatisfied with their purchases if they didn't have to work hard to get it—whether it's a cake that took only two steps to bake instead of five, or a lamp bought online with two quick clicks.

Well-behaved "bébés" and American brats

It doesn't just add value to wait for something. Succumbing to instant gratification makes it impossible to learn how to sit with uncomfortable feelings, which eventually pass, a lesson we're supposed to start teaching our children when they're infants with the Ferber method. By gradually tapering off the number of times they visit fussy children having trouble falling asleep, parents were counseled to use this approach, popularized in the mid-1980s, so that their children would learn to self-soothe. French parents are mystified by the difficulties American parents have with this and other daily challenges, such as allowing children to interrupt phone conversations and dictate mealtimes. Pamela Druckerman writes in *Bringing Up Bébé*, a book about French parenting practices, that French parents are often incredulous that American children can *"n'importe quoi"* or "do whatever they like."[7] Dr. Leonard Sax, the author of *The Collapse of Parenting*, says that parents who fail to help their children restrain themselves and learn deference to adults and rules contribute to a "brattiness" that undermines the ability to be patient.[8]

Patience with one's feelings and the understanding that difficulties pass—and may even result in better long-term outcomes in unexpected areas—is especially challenging among today's adolescents and young adults. Suicides have increased in recent years, which many psychologists attribute to the instant gratification and quick fixes that have become commonplace and lead some to believe their sad feelings are permanent.[9] Just a few months after I spoke to middle school students in Murphy, Texas, one of their school psychologists lamented the suicides of two senior girls in Plano, Texas, who had attended Murphy. She thought that they would have benefitted from hearing my talk and learning about patience and how it can build the grit to withstand difficult times.[10]

Cultivating patience is harder for some children than others. I was first diagnosed with ADHD as a young girl, which was partly why it was so easy for me to tumble into the addiction of bulimia in my teen years. Bulimia presents the almost-magical promise of getting away with eating anything you want without paying the price—except that "almost-magical fixes" always come with some kind of price that costs more than you bargain for. I ultimately had to learn how to cultivate patience to sit with hunger and emotions in order to overcome my eating disorder and tame my natural impulsiveness. So I know it is possible to override the wiring for immediate gratification if you have a goal pulling you forward. In my case, I wanted to be a thriving, healthy woman who wasn't ruled by food, and I did whatever I needed to do on a daily basis to avoid binging and purging or doing something else self-destructive. I later discovered that many of the things that helped me with this task and that led me into thirty years of unbroken recovery are now upheld by research. Living in twenty-four-hour compartments instead of looking for long-term results overnight, being in a community where the desired behavior is the norm, and cultivating gratitude—these are all steps proven to build patience.

TiVo, news crawls, and binge watching

I had the benefit of starting my recovery in the mid-1980s, before the onslaught of personal technology that makes any kind of prolonged effort and concentration difficult. Now, our culture is so wired for instant stimulation that anyone who is trying to cultivate grit in themselves, or their children, is up against daunting challenges. Just take television, for example. News shows now feature "a crawl" of other happenings along the bottom or side of the screen so that we always know what has been discussed, what is being discussed now, and what will be discussed in the next few minutes. And if you don't like what you're watching, your remote control will take you with lightning speed to hundreds of other channels. If you have a TiVo service, you can fast-forward through the recorded commercials and watch only the show itself. And what if you can't wait the millisecond it takes to change a channel to see if your baseball team is winning? Then you can take advantage of the picture-in-picture feature, which allows you to keep a small screen of another channel open on the main screen so that you can watch two shows at once. Finally, you now don't even have to wait for a favorite show to unfold over a season in order to see how a character develops or a plot line unfolds. Netflix routinely dumps an entire season of shows like *House of Cards* onto its service all at once—which has led to conditions jokingly called unseasonal affective disorder and post-binge malaise. Like the food binges I once indulged in that left me with remorse and a hangover, the 61 percent of people who confess to watching multiple episodes, or even an entire season, in one sitting later report sadness, emptiness, and a lack of meaningful purpose.[11]

If it's not the television fostering our impatience, try getting on the telephone. If we call the electric company, we are put on hold with music, advertisements, and a running commentary about the wait itself. When we log in to our email, we are bombarded with messages requesting instant replies, and when we shop online, websites are programmed to create a false sense of urgency, with frequent prompts like "You have five minutes to complete your purchase," "Only two left in stock," or "Sale ends at midnight." Like trained seals, we often do what we're told: we answer that email, respond to that text, and buy that purple spatula, which gives us a false sense of productivity, when in fact all we've done is react to what was in front of us.

Play ball, but do it fast!

It's often said that sports teach character, but it has become harder to learn the virtue of patience there, too. In a global effort to engage younger viewers and participants, sports as diverse as cricket, volleyball, baseball, football, golf, and Formula 1 racing have all found ways to shorten the time needed to watch or play. For example, volleyball players, who are accustomed to celebrating or commiserating every point, which can add fifteen to thirty minutes to a match, are now discouraged from such action.[12] Baseball players cannot move out of the batter's box once they are at the plate, and golfers are now on the clock and penalized for slow play. The world's number-one-ranked golfer, Rory McIlroy, lamented recently that the plummeting interest and participation in golf in England is because "Everything's so instant now, and everyone doesn't have as much time as they used to."[13]

The NCAA Basketball Championship in April 2015 epitomized the changes that have occurred with patience in athletics and how these changes have impacted teamwork and success. The game that spring featured the University of Wisconsin-Madison, headed by coach Bo Ryan, who is known for building a team and cultivating great players over four years, and Duke University, headed by coach Mike Krzyzewski, whose teams are largely populated by "one and done" freshmen who play for one year before leaving for the National

Basketball Association draft. That year, Duke won—a victory that showed why going for individual results and a big payday can be more appealing than working for several years to be part of a greater whole.[14]

"Pencils down" and fast partnership tracks

You don't always have to cultivate patience in the workplace, either. Big changes have been announced on Wall Street and with major banks to keep Millennials from straying after two or three years. Traditionally, the track to becoming a partner involved years of grunt work and hundred-hour workweeks before getting the multi-million-dollar payday, but Millennials don't want to wait, and don't feel the need to compromise family time to achieve their goals. As a result, Citigroup announced in 2016 that it wasn't just planning to help young employees get promoted more quickly, it was also offering a gap year to new hires during which they could work on charitable projects for a smaller salary. JPMorgan Chase & Co. announced a "Pencils Down" initiative allowing bankers to take weekends off. And Goldman Sachs is rejiggering entry-level banking jobs so that less time is spent on spreadsheets and pitch books in favor of more novel work.[15]

While no one would argue that hundred-hour workweeks are appealing or that wanting your job to be more meaningful than boring is bad, the Millennial generation's impatience to get closer to their desired prize a lot sooner and a lot more easily than their parents did is galling to some who feel that this catering is only making problems worse. Some of the Silicon Valley companies that became legendary for removing all nuisances from their young employees' lives—such as standing in line at a barber shop, going to the dry cleaners, and even walking their dogs—are now cutting back on these perks for two reasons: (1) employees begin to take their pampered lives for granted and request more benefits (in an extreme case of not wanting to wait for pleasure, one Silicon Valley startup employee requested that a zip-line be installed from his workplace to the closest bar), and (2) the perks cost too much money.[16]

So what are we supposed to do if patience is in short supply and the cultural triggers around us aren't making it easy to get it? There are glimmers of hope that people want to change, and research is providing clues as well about where we can start to make a difference.

Bayard's story

In the summer of 2015, my youngest child, Bayard, asked me to do something unusual: take him to the phone store to exchange his smartphone for an old-fashioned flip phone. "I'm addicted to this thing," he said, holding it up in resignation. "If I'm not doing something, I look at it to entertain myself, and I'm sick of it. I want to go back to simplicity."

The young man who waited on us at the phone store couldn't believe it when we got there and explained our request. "You are the first person I've ever met who has asked for this," he said to my son, his eyes open in wonderment. "Are you sure?"

Two years later, Bayard is by his own account a different person because of the switch. Although he initially missed the convenience of some of the apps, which allowed him to follow the Washington Nationals or request money from his parents, Bayard says that his newfound freedom from the compulsion to check his phone to see if anyone liked his Instagram post, for example, has made him happier. "I always felt like I was missing out if I wasn't on my phone, but going without it shows me that you really don't miss much," he tells me. He says that he can focus without distraction for longer periods of time, and, most surprisingly, that he enjoys going to baseball games even more now. "I look around between innings and pitching changes, and I can actually observe what's going on and relax instead of staring at my phone," Bayard says.

Although I know most people wouldn't do what Bayard has done, I also know that more and more people are deciding to voluntarily reduce their reliance on constant entertainment and are cultivating patience instead. My daughter, Samantha, was the first to tell me that college students are stacking their phones up at meals in an effort to pay more attention to each other instead of their phones. The first person to grab their phone, apparently, is stuck with the bill for the whole table, which is a powerful motivator to reduce impulsiveness.

Nick's story

I've also found a number of young adults who aspire to careers that won't result in immediate financial gains or instant fame, which gives me hope. I first learned about Nick McGreivy, a classmate of Bayard's, through his mom, Katherine, who came to an event where I was speaking about *Creating Your Best Life*. Afterward, Katherine asked me how to handle Nick's obsession with basketball and his desire to make the middle school team, which she felt might be an unrealistic goal because of Nick's late start in the game and his shorter height. "Am I harming him by encouraging him?" she worried. "Could he have too much grit in a bad way?"

Although he wasn't a natural, Nick's work ethic and disciplined practice ultimately resulted in his making the team. That same focus and mental toughness are what he had to rely on when his charismatic and brilliant father, a physician, died unexpectedly at the end of Nick's high school freshman year. Katherine was left a young widow with four boys, Nick being the oldest.

When I caught up with Nick years later when he was a junior at the University of Pennsylvania, his life was still a study in grit, goal-setting, and future-mindedness. After teaching himself to high-jump in his senior year of high school, he'd made it to the state meet and been recruited by Penn's coach, who allowed him to walk on to the team. His freshman season didn't go as expected, so Nick was cut. Proud of his efforts, nonetheless, Nick decided to tackle organizing a club basketball team, which ran into a number of obstacles, all of which he patiently overcame, one by one. And it shouldn't surprise anyone that Nick hired a jumping coach and worked assiduously in the summer before his senior year to try out again for the Penn team; he jumped a personal best and made the team.

Nick's excitement about working during one summer at Princeton University in their Plasma Physics Laboratory to study nuclear fusion makes sense when you take stock of authentic grit. "A lot of people are cynical about it because it's so hard, but I'm not dissuaded at all that this might not be solved in my lifetime. I think it's really exciting," he says. Like the octogenarians at the Laser Interferometer Gravitational-Wave

Observatory, who spent half of their lives working on Einstein's gravitational waves, Nick has the grit to be in a challenging field solving the hardest of puzzles, something that could never come to those who don't have the patience to work on history-making challenges.[17]

EXERCISE   **Ways to cultivate patience**

- **Play chess.** Board games, particularly games of skill and planning like chess, teach a number of valuable skills, including pattern recognition and patience. Chess yields many positive attributes, such as the need to focus deeply, the ability to visualize the impact a move will have on the future, the patience to wait as a final outcome deliberately and slowly unfolds, and the attention to detail that can make all the difference between winning and losing. Chess is an exercise in planning and patience, honing abilities that are also needed to map out the actions you will need to take to accomplish your long-term life goals.[18] The ability to "focus" and do "deep work" has been described as "the IQ of the 21st century" by Cal Newport, author of *Deep Work,* who says that adults who can focus will be the most prized individuals in coming years.[19]

- **Plant a garden.** You cannot rush the unfolding of a tulip or the ripening of a tomato. Planting a garden and tending to it in the hope that you will be rewarded for your efforts and conscientiousness with beauty and nourishment is one of the time-hallowed ways to learn patience. Dan Buettner, the author of *Blue Zones* and *Thrive,* notes that almost all of the happiest, longest-lived populations in the world have gardens they tend to daily—gardens that produce food and herbs for their healthy meals.[20] The rewards of being in nature and using our hands are also well-known to therapists. Studies show that as little as twenty minutes in nature produces hours of vitality and that using our hands to create something is a sure mood-lifter.[21]

- **Wait in line.** An op-ed piece I read in the *New York Times* pointed to an uptick in the "waiting culture" in some cities, where they have resisted the idea of making it easy to attain something. Several "hot" restaurants that have garnered national attention refuse to take reservations, resulting in multi-hour lines to get a coveted table. Naturally, the fact that you cannot do anything to improve your chances of getting in, other than simply standing in line, gives the restaurants a certain type of cachet and value. If it's worth waiting for, it must be good! The author of this piece also sagely observed that not all waiting is created equal: "Choosing lines wisely, interpreting them, and learning how to enjoy them may be the next skills American consumers everywhere will need to master."[22]

- **Choose to choose in a few weeks.** A unique piece of research on waiting to make a decision—not just waiting in line—found something intriguing. When you decide to defer making a decision until you have slept on it—sometimes for many nights—you learn that patience in making a decision leads to valuing patience itself, and even deciding that long-term rewards are better than short-term payoffs. "People tend to value things more in the present and discount their worth in the future," Ayelet Fishbach, the study author says. "But my research suggests that making people wait to make a decision can improve their patience because the process of waiting makes the reward for waiting seem more valuable."[23]

- **Practice gratitude.** Research on how to curb poor economic decision-making, also called temporal discounting, found that subjects who wrote autobiographical essays describing situations that evoke gratitude were more likely to delay taking an immediate financial reward in favor of a larger one in the future. The novel part of this research is that the study's authors controlled for the emotion of happiness and found that it didn't have the same impact on temporal discounting as gratitude did. ■

EXERCISE   The insight is in the details

Gritty people have to be patient because it takes time for all of the different parts of their goal pursuit to come together. When you have to wait years for the fruits of your labor to pay off, finding joy in small events and savoring them will boost your well-being and sustain your passion, while fine-tuning your ability to extract the best from every detail. The following exercise is based on an assignment Jennifer Roberts, Harvard's Elizabeth Cary Agassiz Professor of the Humanities, uses with her students. It will reward you with a better ability to cultivate patience and to slow down long enough to find the valuable gems in life's details.[24]

Spend thirty minutes observing something without interruption. Take notes about what you see and how it makes you feel. Notice any sensory changes in your body while you observe and contemplate. Take your time. Be slow and deliberate as you gaze, and move on to the next frame of observation only when you feel saturated with the presence of the aspect you focused on previously. Does the object of your attention evoke any similarities to other objects? Do you smell or hear anything that alters your perception? At the end of thirty minutes, write about how the slow process of appraisal is different from a quick look at the same object. Are you aware of any specific differences that make the longer process more valuable or enriching? ■

16

Grit in the Future

've devoted the last few years of my life to thinking about grit, talking about grit, and experimenting with how to help other people understand its importance, create reasons to want to cultivate it, and then have the inner resources to hang in there as they build their own reserves of the character strengths that are most prominent in gritty people. I've sought to embody and broadcast the message that authentic grit is something we can all attain if we are driven toward the right goals for the right reasons. To make the quality as understandable as possible, I've identified the positive and negative types of grit so that people have mental representations of good and bad grit, and more easily know what to do and how to do it for optimal outcomes.

I'm hopeful about the future for a number of reasons, but like any sea change among communities and people, I know it will take self-scrutiny, awareness, planning, commitment, and sacrifice for families, schools, communities, organizations, and countries to turn the tide of visible mediocrity into one of transparent excellence. We will have to stop making it easy for people to succeed at whatever they do—and call it "awesome"—and instead return to celebrating examples of genuinely awe-inspiring behavior that elevates and inspires us. And we can't continue to reward the outrageous behavior of anyone who can broadcast themselves on whatever ubiquitous social-media channel is available. We need to train ourselves to use our precious time and energy to pay attention to quality. Instead of drowning in so much data that we don't have the right filters to know which standards matter, we have to slow down long enough to define what is actually "awesome." And we have to hold ourselves accountable both to be grittier in the pursuit of excellence and to teach others how to be that way, too.

We want grit

No matter where I speak, who I interview, or what I see, I always take away the same message: people are not fooled by flattery, easy wins, or comfortable lives into thinking that they are creating their best selves. On the contrary, unless we are talking about extreme forms of delusion, every single one of us knows excellence when we see it, taste it, feel it, or hear about it, and if we don't have it, we know it deep down and want it to be different. That's why the National Spelling Bee contestants want harder words in the future to avoid ties; that's why the swimmers at my local summer league team tried harder when they saw a record board on the wall; and it's why we all see adults paying large sums of money to learn from successful leaders who promise to teach us what they know about reaching elite status in their field. If we wanted mediocre standards to be our metric, would any of this happen?

I don't think so—but I think a lot of people are lost about how to get started on becoming resilient, excellent, and focused on hard, meaningful goals. That's why the students at Murphy Middle School peppered me with questions and sent me notes about wanting to learn how to "change the channel" in their heads to become grittier after they heard me speak. That's why college students ask me how to define what "hard" is so that they have a metric to measure themselves by. That's why a request on a radio show for volunteers who want to develop better habits was met with thousands and thousands of requests for help.

Become an observer in your own life. Watch how you and others respond when you meet someone who hasn't let obstacles, disappointments, or failure derail their passion; watch your response to those who find ways to persist, achieve, and be grateful for opportunities to excel. We sit up and pay attention when they enter a room, and we gravitate toward them because of their humility, quiet self-assurance, and steely determination. Just like audiences mesmerized by movies showcasing derring-do, we want to know how such men and women all around us overcame the same distractions, temptations, and setbacks that we all face, how they dug deeper and worked harder than anyone thought possible to get somewhere special and meaningful.

People who are the embodiment of deliberate practice, authentic grit, and excellence magnetize us.

What do you stand up for?

I realized one day that whenever I stand up, I do so for the right reasons. I stand up to meet someone for the first time as a sign of respect. I stand up to honor my country when the national anthem plays. I join others in a standing ovation when someone does something so exceptional that I have to go out of my way to express my admiration for their musical ability, athletic prowess, or extraordinary display of character. The expression "stand-up guy" even refers to someone who always does the right thing, though it may not be easy to do so.

I long to be in a world where we aspire to be our best, not because we'll get a trophy but because it will make us better people who set better examples for ourselves and others. I hope that children can play with abandon and without fear or the intrusion of parents and lawyers, so that the lessons of play and competition can build friendships and character. My wish is that we stop protecting our youth from hearing disagreeable thoughts and instead promote critical thinking and intellectual discussion as a way to navigate emotions and perspectives in a fractious world. I pray for a world filled with big goals, fewer excuses and whining, and more post-traumatic resilience and less post-traumatic stress.

Although authentic grit isn't a magic wand and won't solve all problems, I do think making it a priority is the right move for all of us. Too many of us are languishing because we are not shooting for the stars. We are settling for less than what we really want because we don't have the inner resources—and confidence in those resources—to sit through sadness or physical pain when we need to. I see lives change in amazing ways when people summon up the willpower to persevere with hard goals. I see them create teams of supportive friendships and serve others with a passionate purpose. I see regret and misery when people languish and play small.

Although every generation longs for "the good old days," it's not hard to see why you will need to get more grit if you are to survive and thrive in this uncertain world. We are facing environmental challenges that are putting entire countries at risk: global warming, rising oceans, and earthquakes make geographical stability impossible. The wild gyrations in financial markets and international political movements have thrust the world into scary situations, and the unending reports of warfare and terrorism have put us all on edge. Being soft, anxious, and hiding in "safe spaces" simply won't cut it, so becoming more courageous, resolute, and positive is necessarily going to be our best option.

My hope is that you will use this book, with its ideas, stories, suggestions, and exercises, as a resource to craft the grittiest life possible. Change starts with each one of us doing our best, one day at a time, patiently and with humility, and when we do it in concert with others, we get collectively stronger and more powerful. And if we can do that, I hope that the contentment and happiness we all seek will fill our lives, our families, our communities, and our countries with the hard-earned pride that only our best and most steadfast efforts can give us.

If I could get grit, you can, too, and it's never too late to get started down the path that will take you exactly as far as you want. Take the steps necessary to fill your life with authentic grit, and I promise you that you will not only never regret it, you'll also have nothing but respect for yourself when you're looking back and asking yourself what you did to make a difference in your own life, and in the lives of others, while you could.

Acknowledgments

alth012ugh I've written a number of books since the 1980s, *Getting Grit* was truly a lesson in having grit because of the many obstacles I had to overcome to cross the finish line. And since you can't cultivate authentic grit without the support of a team around you, I have a number of people to thank who make up my fantastic team.

My life took a decidedly positive turn when I returned to the University of Pennsylvania to get a master's degree in applied positive psychology in 2005. During my year in that pioneering class, I was lit up with an unquenchable thirst to learn and share as much as I could about the new science of happiness, which provided me with a new professional purpose. While there, I was introduced to Angela Duckworth's fledgling work on grit, which she later insisted I turn into a full-fledged book. Ten years later, her support for this book, as her own grit book soared to the top of the bestseller lists, was both kind and generous.

Stacey Colino got the ball rolling when she interviewed me in 2013 and asked, "What is your next book about?" When I told her I didn't know, she said, "I do. It has to be about grit because every book you've written has the thread of grit running through it." She was right, and since that day I've been committed to getting this book done.

In January 2016, I decided to cancel all of my coaching clients and professional engagements and go away and do nothing but focus on organizing my book. My lifelong friend and childhood swimming partner, Kelly Parker Palace, and her husband, Mark, graciously opened their spectacular oceanfront Florida home to me for almost a month, and I benefitted greatly from our nightly debates and their cogent comments about my grit definitions.

Megan McDonough of the Wholebeing Institute suggested that Sounds True consider my manuscript in April 2016 when a hole unexpectedly opened up in their 2017 publication list. That kind suggestion led me to the wonderful team of Jennifer Brown and Haven Iverson, who took the leap, made an offer, and brought me and my book into the fold. Vesela Simic quickly became my trusted partner and calm editor as she wove her magic and made the book sparkle; it is vastly better because she brought her life experiences and wisdom to the editing process.

My virtual mastermind group of Margarita Tarragona, Louisa Jewell, and David Pollay has given me new ideas and supportive cheerleading every month for several years. This journey would have been much harder without them.

My agent and his wife, Ivor and Ronnie Whitson, are unfailingly optimistic, classy, and professional regardless of what we're going through, and I pinch myself often that I am lucky enough to be represented by Ivor. Michele Lucia of ADL Speaker Management and her assistant, Nancy Winkler, came into my life just as I committed to getting the book done, and without them, I never would have been able to satisfy my speaking commitments and appearance requests, stay organized, or keep going during some exceptionally challenging months.

I have come to rely heavily on a coterie of professionals who make me better at what I do, from head to toe, and who bring their special magic to some part of my life. They include Marina Alterman, Tasha Bates Bernard, Ruth Benevides, Olena Levanda, Soroor Mohammad, Lisa Oswald, Manuela Salguero, Paul Thomas, Bill Whited, and Sormeh Youssefieh.

Karen Collias entered my life when our daughters became friends twenty years ago. Our friendship continues to deepen, and her brilliant observations always make me think harder and laugh louder. My godmother, Pat Griffith, a formidable and legendary journalist in her own right, has always encouraged and loved me, starting within days of my birth. Judy Feld has coached me for nearly two decades, and her guidance and belief in my work has brought incomparable value, not to mention unexpected insights that have led me to positively pivot in strategic ways at just the right moment. Debbie Mahony has designed and maintained all my websites and fulfilled my many graphic needs—and so much more—for over a decade, and her sister, Donna del Giudice, runs my back office and keeps all of the numbers straight. Mario Carlo Severo does all of my research gathering from distant European labs within hours of my emailed requests. And last but not least, my L4 Masters swim teammates are my cheerful, curious 4:45 a.m. friends, who start most of my days with high energy, laughter, and positive activity.

Finally, it takes authentic grit to be married for three and a half decades and to raise three children while juggling the responsibilities of motherhood and being a solopreneur, but my family has given me a solid rock to build upon, plus the cushion of fun, laughter, and wry observations. A big hug and kiss to my husband, Haywood Miller, who understands and supports my quirky writing habits of disappearing into random bargain hotels on weekends to create a cone of creative silence, and also to my three amazing children, Haywood IV, Samantha, and Bayard, whose lives are reflected in these pages and who shared their historical, political, and sports ideas with me whenever I needed examples to flesh out my points, and who know how to restore my mood with emojis and ridiculous animal videos when I need to take a break and laugh.

Thank you to everyone who isn't named here, but who has played some role in helping me make a difference, and hopefully make the world a happier, grittier, and more proactive place.

Notes

Chapter 1   Can You Spell G-R-I-T?

1. Olivia B. Waxman, "Past Winners of the Scripps National Spelling Bee: Where They Are Now," *TIME,* May 25, 2016, time.com/4344080/scripps-national-spelling-bee-winners-where-are-they-now/.

2. Paul Tough, "To Help Kids Thrive, Coach Their Parents," *New York Times,* May 21, 2016, nytimes.com/2016/05/22/opinion/sunday/to-help-kids-thrive-coach-their-parents.html?_r=0.

3. Joel Stein, "Millennials: The Me Me Me Generation," *TIME,* May 20, 2013, time.com/247/millennials-the-me-me-me-generation/.

4. Sumathi Reddi, "Playing It Too Safe?," *Wall Street Journal,* November 19, 2012, wsj.com/articles/SB10001424127887323362290457812906 3506832312; Janny Scott, "When Child's Play Is Too Simple: Experts Criticize Safety-Conscious Recreation as Boring," *New York Times,* July 15, 2000, nytimes.com/2000/07/15/arts/when-child-s-play-too-simple-experts-criticize-safety-conscious-recreation.html?_r=0; Rebecca Sheir, "For Kids This Summer, How Safe Is Too Safe?," *All Things Considered,* National Public Radio, July 7, 2013, npr.org/templates/story/story.php?storyId=199773134.

5. Robert J. Samuelson, "The start-up slump," *Washington Post,* December 16, 2015, washingtonpost.com/opinions/the-start-up-slump/2015/12/16/91ded2dc-a40e-11e5-b53d-972e2751f433_story.html?utm_term=.2e03b4f0b8db; Ibid, "Where have all the entrepreneurs gone (continued)?," *Washington Post,* August 13, 2014, washingtonpost.com/opinions/robert-samuelson-where-have-all-the-entrepreneurs-gone-continued/2014/08/13/2010fa54-2318-11e4-86ca-6f03cbd15c1a_story.html?utm_term=.8860d526b165.

6. Matt Bonesteel, "SMU women's coach says kids these days drove her into retirement," *Washington Post,* February 16, 2016, washingtonpost.com/news/early-lead/wp/2016/02/26/smu-womens-coach-says-kids-these-days-drove-her-into-retirement/.

7. Martin E. P. Seligman, *Flourish: A Visionary New Understanding of Happiness and Well-being* (New York: Free Press, 2011), 71–72.

8. Edwin A. Locke and Gary P. Latham, "Building a practically useful theory of goal setting and task motivation: A 35-year odyssey," *American Psychologist* 57, no. 9 (September 2002): 705–717; Richard M. Ryan and Edward L. Deci, "Self-determination theory and the facilitation of intrinsic motivation, social development, and well-being," *American Psychologist* 55, no. 1 (January 2000): 68–78.

9. Association for Psychological Science, "To make one happy, make one busy," ScienceDaily.com, July 29, 2010, sciencedaily.com/releases/2010/07/100729101615.htm; Rachel Feintzeig, "Being Busy Isn't So Bad After All," *Wall Street Journal,* July 17, 2014, blogs.wsj.com/atwork/2014/07/17/the-benefits-of-being-busy/.

10. Ryan T. Howell, David Chenot, Graham Hill, and Colleen J. Howell, "Momentary Happiness: The Role of Psychological Need Satisfaction," *Journal of Happiness Studies* 12, no.1 (March 2011): 1–15.

11. Kennon M. Sheldon, Paul E. Jose, Todd B. Kashdan, and Aaron Jarden, "Personality, Effective Goal-Striving, and Enhanced Well-Being: Comparing 10 Candidate Personality Strengths," *Personality and Social Psychology Bulletin* 41, no. 4 (April 2015): 575–585.

12. Carol Dweck, "The power of believing that you can improve," TED video, 10:20, filmed at TEDxNorrköping on November 2014, ted.com/talks/carol_dweck_the_power_of_believing_that_you_can_improve?language=en.

13. A. W. Blanchfield, J. Hardy, H. M. DeMorree, W. Staiano, and S. M. Marcora, "Talking yourself out of exhaustion: the effects of self-talk on endurance performance," *Med Sci Sports Exercise* 46, no. 5 (2014): 998–1007.

14. Ruud Custers and Henk Aarts, "Positive affect as implicit motivator: On the nonconscious operation of behavioral goals," *Journal of Personality and Social Psychology* 89, no. 2 (2005): 129–142.

15. Rodney Brookes, "Living longer means a second chance at those life decisions you now regret," *Washington Post,* June 13, 2016, washingtonpost.com/news/get-there/wp/2016/06/13/living-longer-means-a-second-chance-at-those-life-decisions-you-now-regret/.

16. Kevin McSpadden, "You Now Have a Shorter Attention Span Than a Goldfish," *TIME,* May 14, 2015, time.com/3858309/attention-spans-goldfish/.

17. "University of Texas at Austin 2014 Commencement Address – Admiral William H. McRaven," YouTube video, 19:26, posted by "Texas Exes," May 9, 2014, youtube.com/watch?v=pxBQLFLei70.

Chapter 2 When Grit Is Gone: Wood Chips, Comfort Pigs, and Cuddlers

1. Laurie Los, "Montgomery Square heroes give back," Gazette.net, July 23, 2003, gazette.net/gazette_archive/2003/200330/damascus/sports/169168-1.html.

2. M. W. Lilliquist, H. P. Nair, F. Gonzalez-Lima, and A. Amsel, "Extinction after regular and irregular reward schedules in the infant rat: Influence of age and training duration," *Developmental Psychobiology* 34, no. 1 (January 1999): 57–70.

3. Kevin Helliker, "The Slowest Generation: Younger Athletes Are Racing With Less Concern About Time," *Wall Street Journal,* September 19, 2013, wsj.com/news/articles/SB10001424127887324807704579085084130007974.

4. Charlie Boss, "Best of class? In Dublin, 222 grads tie," *Columbus Dispatch,* June 3, 2015, dispatch.com/content/stories/local/2015/06/03/best-of-class-in-dublin-222-grads-tie.html.

5. Janell Ross, "We should stop asking why Indian Americans are so good at spelling bees. Here's why," *Washington Post,* May 29, 2015, washingtonpost.com/news/the-fix/wp/2015/05/29/we-should-stop-asking-why-indian-americans-are-so-good-at-spelling-bees-heres-why/.

6. Douglas Ernst, "School bars honors insignia at graduation to protect underachievers' feelings," *Washington Times,* June 1, 2016, washingtontimes.com/news/2016/jun/1/school-bars-national-honor-society-insignia-at-gra/; Katherine Timpf, "School Board Votes to Ban Having Valedictorians Because the 'Competition' is 'Unhealthy,'" *National Review,* May 19, 2016, nationalreview.com/article/435639/school-board-votes-ban-having-valedictorians-because-competition-unhealthy.

7. Reynol Junco, "Student class standing, Facebook use, and academic performance," *Journal of Applied Developmental Psychology* 36 (January-February 2015): 18–29.

8. Max Roosevelt, "Student Expectations Seen as Causing Grade Disputes," *New York Times,* February 17, 2009, nytimes.com/2009/02/18/education/18college.html?_r=0.

9. Meg P. Bernhard, "Princeton grade deflation reversal disappoints some here," *Harvard Crimson,* October 9, 2014, thecrimson.com/article/2014/10/9/princeton-grade-deflation-reversal/; Christopher Healy and Stuart Rojstaczer, "Where A Is Ordinary: The Evolution of American College and University Grading, 1940–2009," *Teachers College Record* 114, no. 7 (2012).

10. Meg P. Bernhard, "Princeton grade deflation reversal disappoints some here."

11. Emily Esfahani Smith, "Profile in Courage: Harvey Mansfield," *Defining Ideas: A Hoover Institution Journal,* December 13, 2010, hoover.org/research/profile-courage-harvey-mansfield.

12. Ulrich Boser and Lindsay Rosenthal, "Do Schools Challenge Our Students? What Student Surveys Tell Us About the State of Education in the United States," Center for American Progress, July 10, 2012, americanprogress.org/issues/education/reports/2012/07/10/11913/do-schools-challenge-our-students/.

13. B. Brett Finlay and Marie-Claire Arrieta, "Get Your Children Good and Dirty," *Wall Street Journal,* September 15, 2016, wsj.com/articles/get-your-children-good-and-dirty-1473950250.

14. Maria Guido, "Letters Sent To Parents Offers Fake Report Card Options For Kids," ScaryMommy.com, scarymommy.com/letter-sent-to-parents-offers-fake-report-card-option-for-kids/.

15. Edward Schlosser, "I'm a liberal professor, and my liberal students terrify me," Vox.com, June 3, 2015, vox.com/2015/6/3/8706323/college-professor-afraid.

16. Dick Hilker, "Hilker: On college campuses, it's disinvitation season," *Denver Post,* May 6, 2016, http://www.denverpost.com/2016/05/06/hilker-on-college-campuses-its-disinvitation-season/.

17. Soo Youn, "Antonin Scalia: liberal clerks reflect on the man they knew and admired," *The Guardian,* February 15, 2016, theguardian.com/law/2016/feb/15/antonin-scalia-supreme-court-justice-liberal-clerks-reflect.

18. Greg Lukianoff and Jonathan Haidt, "The Coddling of the American Mind," *The Atlantic,* September 2015, theatlantic.com/magazine/archive/2015/09/the-coddling-of-the-american-mind/399356/.

19. Judith Shulevitz, "In College and Hiding from Scary Ideas," *New York Times,* March 21, 2015, nytimes.com/2015/03/22/opinion/sunday/judith-shulevitz-hiding-from-scary-ideas.html?_r=0.

20. Dr. Everett Piper, "This Is Not a Day Care. It's a University!," Oklahoma Wesleyan University, okwu.edu/blog/2015/11/this-is-not-a-day-care-its-a-university/.

21. Anemona Hartocollis, "College Students Protest, Alumni's Fondness Fades and Checks Shrink," *New York Times,* August 4, 2016, nytimes.com/2016/08/05/us/college-protests-alumni-donations.html.

22. Leonor Vivanco and Dawn Rhodes, "U. of C. tells incoming freshmen it does not support 'trigger warnings' or 'safe spaces,'" *Chicago Tribune,* August 25, 2016, chicagotribune.com/news/local/breaking/ct-university-of-chicago-safe-spaces-letter-met-20160825-story.html.

23. Jan Hoffman, "Campuses Debate Rising Demands for 'Comfort Animals,'" *New York Times,* October 4, 2015, nytimes.com/2015/10/05/us/four-legged-roommates-help-with-the-stresses-of-campus-life.html.

24. Emanuella Grinberg, "Airline: 'Emotional support' pig kicked off flight for being disruptive," CNN.com, December 1, 2014, cnn.com/2014/11/30/travel/emotional-support-pig-booted-flight/index.html.

25. Yanan Wang, "Someone just used a federal law to bring a live turkey on a Delta flight," *Washington Post,* January 15, 2016, washingtonpost.com/news/morning-mix/wp/2016/01/15/someone-just-used-a-federal-law-to-bring-a-live-turkey-on-a-delta-flight/.

26. Stephanie Armour, "Professional Cuddlers Embrace More Clients," *Wall Street Journal,* January 8, 2015, wsj.com/articles/professional-cuddlers-embrace-more-clients-1420759074.

Chapter 3 How Do You Start Getting More Grit?

1. Hengchen Dai, Katherine L. Milkman, and Jason Riis, "The Fresh Start Effect: Temporal Landmarks Motivate Aspirational Behavior," *Management Science* 60, vol. 10, accessed at pubsonline.informs.org/doi/abs/10.1287/mnsc.2014.1901.

2. Pelin Kesebir, "Virtues: Irreplaceable Tools to Cultivate Your Well-Being," Center for Healthy Minds – University of Wisconsin-Madison, August 2016 newsletter, centerhealthyminds.org/join-the-movement/virtues-irreplaceable-tools-to-cultivate-your-well-being.

3. Charlie Wells, "The Hidden Reasons People Spend Too Much," *Wall Street Journal,* November 2, 2015, wsj.com/articles/the-hidden-reasons-people-spend-too-much-1446433200; Mike Bundrant, "Negative Future Perception and the Vicious Cycle of Depression," *NLP Discoveries with Mike Bundrant* (blog), *PsychCentral,* July 6, 2015, blogs.psychcentral.com/nlp/2015/07/negative-future-perception-and-the-vicious-cycle-of-depression/.

4. J. L. Austenfeld and A. L. Stanton, "Writing about emotions versus goals: Effects on hostility and medical care utilization moderated by emotional approach coping processes," *British Journal of Health Psychology* 13, Part 1 (2008): 35–38; J. L. Austenfeld, A. M. Paolo, and A. L. Stanton, "Effects of writing about emotions versus goals on psychological and physical health among third-year medical students," *Journal of Personality* 74, no. 1 (2006): 267–286; Laura A. King, "The health benefits of writing about life goals," *Personality and Social Psychology Bulletin* 27, no. 7 (2001): 798–807; Y. M. Meevissen, M. L. Peters, and H. J. Alberts, "Become more optimistic by imagining a best possible self: Effects of a two week

intervention," *Journal of Behavior Therapy and Experimental Psychiatry* 42, vol. 3 (2011): 371–378; M. L. Peters, I. K. Flink, K. Boersma, and S. J. Linton, "Manipulating optimism: Can imagining a best possible self be used to increase positive future expectancies?," *Journal of Positive Psychology* 5, no. 3: 204–211; Christopher Peterson and Martin E. P. Seligman, *Character Strengths and Virtues: A Handbook and Classification* American Psychological Association/Oxford University Press, New York and Washington, DC: 2004; L. B. Shapira and M. Mongrain, "The benefits of self-compassion and optimism exercises for individuals vulnerable to depression," *Journal of Positive Psychology* 5, no. 5 (2010): 377–389; K. M. Sheldon and S. Lyubomirsky, "How to increase and sustain positive emotion: The effects of expressing gratitude and visualizing best possible selves," *Journal of Positive Psychology* 1, no. 2 (2006): 73–82.

5. Anya Kamenetz, "The Writing Assignment That Changes Lives," National Public Radio, July 10, 2015, npr.org/sections/ed/2015/07/10/419202925/the-writing-assignment-that-changes-lives.

Chapter 4   Authentic Grit: What Is It?

1. Carrie Rickey, "Perfectly Happy, Even Without Happy Endings," *New York Times*, January 13, 2012, nytimes.com/2012/01/15/movies/lindsay-doran-examines-what-makes-films-satisfying.html.

Chapter 5   Good Grit: Mt. Rushmore, Mt. Olympus, Celebrity, and Ordinary

1. Norman Lebrecht, "How Harry Saved Reading," *Wall Street Journal*, July 9, 2011, wsj.com/articles/SB10001424052702304584004576419742308635716.

Chapter 6   Bad Grit: Faux, Stubborn, and Selfie

1. Michael Taylor, "Tracking Down False Heroes / Medal of Honor recipients go after impostors," SFGATE.com, May 31, 1999, sfgate.com/news/article/Tracking-Down-False-Heroes-Medal-of-Honor-2928051.php.

2. Ibid.

3. Michael Barbaro, "Donald Trump Likens His Schooling to Military Service in Book," *New York Times*, September 8, 2015, nytimes.com/2015/09/09/us/politics/donald-trump-likens-his-schooling-to-military-service-in-book.html.

4. Peter Botte, "No Juice! Baseball Hall of Fame voters tough on Barry Bonds, Roger Clemens and steroid era players again," *New York*

Daily News, January 7, 2016, nydailynews.com/sports/baseball/
no-juice-hall-fame-voters-tough-steroid-era-article-1.2488327.

5. Robert Craddock, "Michelle Smith—the most intriguing Olympic
story never told," News.com.au, July 21, 2012, news.com.au/sport/
michelle-smith-the-most-intriguing-olympic-story-never-told/story-
fndpv1cc-1226431290041; Jere Longman, "SWIMMING; Olympic
Swimming Star Banned; Tampering with Drug Test Cited," *New York
Times,* August 7, 1998, nytimes.com/1998/08/07/sports/swimming-
olympic-swimming-star-banned-tampering-with-drug-test-cited.html.

6. Lynn Zinser, "The Guy Who Would Never Give Up," *New York Times,*
August 24, 2012, nytimes.com/2012/08/25/sports/reaction-to-lance-
armstrong-conceding-defeat-leading-off.html.

7. David Roberts and Joanna Williams, "Academic Integrity: Exploring
Tensions Between Perception and Practice in the Contemporary
University" (working paper, Society for Research into Higher Education,
University of Kent, Canterbury, 2014).

8. Joe Stephens and Mary Pat Flaherty, "How the 'queen' of high school
rowing left a Virginia nonprofit treading water," *Washington Post,* October
30, 2013, washingtonpost.com/investigations/how-the-queen-of-high-
school-rowing-left-a-virginia-nonprofit-treading-water/2013/10/26/
fce08aac-254a-11e3-b3e9-d97fb087acd6_story.html.

9. Lisa D. Ordóñez, Maurice E. Schweitzer, Adam D. Galinsky, and Max
H. Bazerman, "Goals Gone Wild: The Systematic Side Effects of Over-
Prescribing Goal Setting" (working paper, Harvard Business School,
Boston, 2009).

10. Robert Sherefkin, "Lee Iacocca's Pinto: A fiery failure," *Automotive News,*
June 16, 2003, autonews.com/article/20030616/SUB/306160770/
lee-iacoccas-pinto:-a-fiery-failure.

11. CBC News, "Canadian Everest victim used inexperienced company,
lacked oxygen," CBCNews.com, September 13, 2012, cbc.ca/news/
canada/exclusive-canadian-everest-victim-used-inexperienced-company-
lacked-oxygen-1.1195149.

12. Wiktionary, s.v. "summit fever," last modified January 17, 2016,
en.wiktionary.org/wiki/summit_fever.

13. Wiktionary, s.v. "nitrogen narcosis," last modified April 26, 2016,
en.wiktionary.org/wiki/nitrogen_narcosis.

14. Kim Carollo and ABC News Medical Unit, "Thirteen
University of Iowa Football Players Hospitalized," ABCNews.
com, January 28, 2011, abcnews.go.com/Health/

university-iowa-football-players-hospitalized-muscle-condition/ story?id=12780810.

15. Lindsay Crouse, "His Strength Sapped, Top Marathoner Ryan Hall Decides to Stop," *New York Times,* January 15, 2016, nytimes.com/2016/01/17/ sports/ryan-hall-fastest-us-distance-runner-is-retiring.html.

16. Christopher Clarey, "For Williams, Triumph and Pain Come at One Speed," *New York Times,* February 2, 2015, nytimes.com/2015/02/03/ sports/tennis/no-quit-for-serena-williams-is-a-double-edged-sword.html.

17. Wikipedia, s.v. "loss aversion," last modified November 3, 2016, en.wikipedia.org/wiki/loss_aversion.

18. Remarks made at University of Pennsylvania MAPP summit, October 18, 2015.

19. Phil Bronstein, "The Man Who Killed Osama bin Laden . . . Is Screwed," *Esquire,* February 11, 2013, esquire.com/news-politics/a26351/ man-who-shot-osama-bin-laden-0313/.

20. Jasper Hamill, "'I know how to defend myself,' Navy SEAL Robert O'Neill warns ISIS after extremist death threats," *Mirror Online,* October 7, 2015, mirror.co.uk/news/technology-science/ technology/i-know-how-defend-myself-6592347.

21. Nina Mandell, "Johnny Manziel flashed the money sign after being drafted by the Browns," *USA Today Sports,* May 8, 2014, ftw.usatoday. com/2014/05/johnny-manziel-money-sign.

22. *A Season with Notre Dame Football,* season 1, episode 1, September 8, 2015, sho.com/a-season-with/season/1/episode/1.

Chapter 8 Building Passion to Fuel Purpose

1. Pamela Druckerman, "Learning How to Exert Self-Control," *New York Times,* September 12, 2014, nytimes.com/2014/09/14/opinion/sunday/ learning-self-control.html.

2. Christopher Ingraham, "This is what 5.8 million failures look like," *Washington Post,* July 8, 2016, washingtonpost.com/news/wonk/ wp/2016/07/08/this-is-what-5-8-million-failures-look-like/.

3. Jennifer Maloney and Megumi Fujikawa, "Marie Kondo and the Cult of Tidying Up," *Wall Street Journal,* February 26, 2015, wsj.com/articles/ marie-kondo-and-the-tidying-up-trend-1424970535.

4. Fred Barnes, "The Savviest Lobbyist," *Wall Street Journal,* July 10, 2016, wsj.com/articles/the-savviest-lobbyist-1468183798.

Chapter 9 Happiness

1. Scott Stossel, "What Makes Us Happy, Revisited," *The Atlantic,* April 24, 2013.

2. Sue Shellenbarger, "To Stop Procrastinating, Look to Science of Mood Repair," *Wall Street Journal,* January 7, 2014.

3. Susan Dominus, "Is Giving the Secret to Getting Ahead?," *New York Times,* March 27, 2013.

4. Lucette Lagnado, "Can Meditation Help Pain after Surgery?," *Wall Street Journal,* September 19, 2016.

5. Redzo Mujcic and Andrew J. Oswald, "Evolution of Well-Being and Happiness After Increases in Consumption of Fruit and Vegetables," *American Journal of Public Health* 106, no. 8 (August 2016): 1504–1510.

6. Paul Piff and Dacher Keltner, "Why Do We Experience Awe?," *New York Times,* May 22, 2015.

Chapter 10 Goal Setting

1. Claire Cain Miller and Nick Bilton, "Google's Lab of Wildest Dreams," *New York Times,* November 13, 2011.

2. A. Bandura, "Self-efficacy," in *Encyclopedia of Human Behavior,* vol. 4, ed. V. S. Ramachandran (New York: Academic Press, 1994): 71–81. (Reprinted in *Encyclopedia of Mental Health,* ed. H. Friedman [San Diego: Academic Press, 1998].)

3. Kelly Seegers, "Katie Ledecky visits Stone Ridge and Little Flower before heading to Stanford," CatholicStandard.com, September 9, 2016, cathstan. org/Content/News/Schools/Article/Katie-Ledecky-visits-Stone-Ridge-and-Little-Flower-before-heading-to-Stanford/2/21/7240.

4. S. L. Price, "Back to her roots: How Katie Ledecky became so dominant in the pool," *Sports Illustrated,* June 1, 2016, si.com/olympics/2016/06/01/olympics-2016-road-to-rio-katie-ledecky-swimming.

5. Kamenetz, "The Writing Assignment That Changes Lives." (see chap. 3, n. 5)

6. Dominique Morisano, Jacob B. Hirsh, Jordan B. Peterson, Robert O. Pihl, and Bruce M. Shore, "Setting, elaborating and reflecting on personal goals improves academic performance," *Journal of Applied Psychology* 95, no. 2 (March 2010): 255–264.

7. Chana R. Schoenberger, "Can't Stand Your Commute? It's All in Your Head," *Wall Street Journal,* May 30, 2016.

8. Tara Parker-Pope, "Writing Your Way to Happiness," *New York Times,* January 19, 2015, well.blogs.nytimes.com/2015/01/19/writing-your-way-to-happiness/.

Chapter 11   Self-Regulation

1. Michael Lewis, "Obama's Way," *Vanity Fair,* October 2012.

2. Rebecca Klein, "Why Schools Should Pay More Attention to Students' Grit and Self-Control," HuffingtonPost.com, December 30, 2014, huffingtonpost.com/2014/12/30/non-cognitive-skills_n_6392582.html.

3. Cal Newport, *Deep Work: Rules for Focused Success in a Distracted World* (New York: Grand Central Publishing, 2016).

4. John Tierney, "Do You Suffer from Decision Fatigue?," *New York Times,* August 17, 2011.

5. Kirsten Weir, "What You Need to Know About Willpower: The Psychological Science of Self-Control," American Psychological Association, 2012, apa.org/helpcenter/willpower.pdf.

6. Justin Caba, "Midlife Crisis: Why Middle-Aged Women Have the Highest Rate of Depression," MedicalDaily.com, December 4, 2014, medicaldaily.com/midlife-crisis-why-middle-aged-women-have-highest-rate-depression-313082.

7. Joel Achenbach, "Life expectancy for white females in U.S. suffers rare decline," *Washington Post,* April 20, 2016.

8. Laura A. King and Courtney Raspin, "Lost and found possible selves, subjective well-being, and ego depletion in divorced women," *Journal of Personality* 72, no. 3 (June 2004): 603–632.

9. Ekaterina Walter, "What Your Conference Room Names Say About Your Company Culture," Inc.com, October 21, 2014, inc.com/ekaterina-walter/what-your-conference-room-names-say-about-your-company-culture.html.

10. K. Hardcastle, K. Hughes, O. Sharples, and M. Bellis, "Trends in alcohol portrayal in popular music: A longitudinal analysis of the UK charts," *Psychology of Music* 43, no. 3 (May 2015): 321–332.

11. "Inaction-related words in our environment can unconsciously influence our self-control," MedicalNewsToday.com, published August 11, 2013, medicalnewstoday.com/releases/264604.php.

12. Lisa Belkin, "In Praise of Roughhousing," *New York Times,* June 14, 2011.

13. Bradley Staats and David M. Upton, "Lean Knowledge Work," *Harvard Business Review,* October 2011.

Chapter 12   Risk-Taking

1. Pat Forde, "Katie Ledecky set to chase Olympic history," Yahoo Sports, May 28, 2015, sports.yahoo.com/news/

katie-ledecky-now-set-to-chase-olympic-history-after-surprising-gold-in-2012-040626612-olympics.html.

2. Scott Stump, "'Magnificent Seven' US gymnastics team revisits 1996 Olympic triumph," Today.com, July 12, 2016, today.com/news/magnificent-seven-us-gymnastics-team-revisits-1996-olympic-triumph-t100730.

3. Interview with the author, March 25, 2008.

4. Ruth Chang, "How to Make Hard Choices" (transcript), TED, June 2014, ted.com/talks/ruth_chang_how_to_make_hard_choices/transcript.

5. Emma Fierberg and Alana Kakoyiannis, "Learning to celebrate failure at a young age led to this billionaire's success," *Business Insider,* July 11, 2016, businessinsider.com/sara-blakely-spanx-ceo-offers-advice-redefine-failure-retail-2016-7.

6. Leslie Kwoh, "Memo to Staff: Take More Risks: CEOs Urge Employees to Embrace Failure and Keep Trying," *Wall Street Journal,* updated March 20, 2013, wsj.com/articles/SB100014241278873236396045783703839 39044780.

7. Carl Richards, "Hesitant to Make That Big Life Change? Permission Granted," *New York Times,* August 15, 2016, nytimes.com/2016/08/16/your-money/hesitant-to-make-that-big-life-change-permission-granted.html?_r=0.

8. Harry T. Reis, Shannon M. Smith, Cheryl L. Carmichael, Peter A. Caprariello, Fen-Fang Tsai, Amy Rodrigues, and Michael R. Maniaci, "Are you happy for me? How sharing positive events with others provides personal and interpersonal benefits," *Journal of Personality and Social Psychology* 99, no. 2 (August 2010): 311–329; Shelly L. Gable, Harry T. Reis, Emily A. Impett, and Evan R. Asher, "What do you do when things go right? The intrapersonal and interpersonal benefits of sharing positive events," *Journal of Personality and Social Psychology* 87, no. 2 (August 2004): 228–245.

9. Dara Torres with Elizabeth Weil, *Age Is Just a Number: Achieve Your Dreams at Any Stage in Your Life* (New York: Three Rivers Press, 2010).

Chapter 13 Humility

1. Jim Collins, "Level 5 Leadership: The Triumph of Humility and Fierce Resolve," *Harvard Business Review,* July–August 2005.

2. Peter L. Samuelson, Matthew J. Jarvinen, Thomas B. Paulus, Ian M. Church, Sam A. Hardy, and Justin L. Barrett, "Implicit theories of intellectual virtues and vices: A focus on intellectual

humility," *Journal of Positive Psychology* 10, vol. 5 (May 2014), doi: 10.1080/17439760.2014.967802.

3. Ibid.

4. Ibid.

5. Don Emerson Davis, Jr., and Joshua N. Hook, "Measuring Humility and Its Positive Effects," *Observer* 28, no. 8 (October 2013), psychologicalscience.org/publications/observer/2013/october-13/measuring-humility-and-its-positive-effects.html.

6. Adam Bryant, "Google's Quest to Build a Better Boss," *New York Times*, March 12, 2011, nytimes.com/2011/03/13/business/13hire.html.

7. Baylor University, "The Top Athletes Display Humility, Says Researcher," Newswise.com, October 22, 2006, newswise.com/articles/the-top-athletes-display-humility-says-researcher.

8. "'Persist, Persist, Persist!' This Student's Speech Will CHANGE YOUR LIFE!", YouTube video, 7:39, posted by "Alvernia University," January 6, 2015, youtube.com/watch?v=GUZS-ScfuSQ.

9. Junior Bernard (Haitian immigrant and graduate of Alvernia University), interview with Caroline Adams Miller, February 14, 2016.

10. Susan Dominus, "Is Giving the Secret to Getting Ahead?," *New York Times*, March 27, 2013.

11. Jordan Paul LaBouff, Wade C. Rowatt, Meghan Johnson Shen, Jo-Ann Tsang, and Grace McCullough Willerton, "Humble persons are more helpful than less humble persons: Evidence from three studies," *Journal of Positive Psychology* 7, no. 1 (January 2012): 16–29.

12. Bradley P. Owens, Michael D. Johnson, and Terence R. Mitchell, "Expressed Humility in Organizations: Implications for Performance, Teams, and Leadership," *Organization Science* 24, no. 5 (September–October 2013): 1517–1538.

13. Christopher Harress, "The Law of Jante: How a Swedish Cultural Principle Drives Ikea, Ericsson, and Volvo, and Beat the Financial Crisis," *International Business Times*, August 23, 2014, ibtimes.com/law-jante-how-swedish-cultural-principle-drives-ikea-ericsson-volvo-beat-financial-1397589.

14. Michael Booth, "The Danish Don't Have the Secret to Happiness," *The Atlantic*, January 30, 2015, TheAtlantic.com/health/archive/2015/01/the-danish-dont-have-the-secret-to-happiness/384930/.

15. Douglas Ernst, "School bars honors insignia at graduation to protect underachievers' feelings." (see chap. 2, n. 6)

16. Katherine Timpf, "School Board Votes to Ban Having Valedictorians Because the 'Competition' is 'Unhealthy.'" (see chap. 2, n. 6)

17. Kate Murphy, "What Selfie Sticks Really Tell Us About Ourselves," *New York Times,* August 8, 2015, NYTimes.com/2015/08/09/sunday-review/what-selfie-sticks-really-tell-us-about-ourselves.html?_r=0.

Chapter 14   Perseverance

1. Paul Thomas (founder of Tong Leong School of Martial Arts), interview with Caroline Adams Miller, May 25, 2016.

2. William James, "The Energies of Men," *Science* 25, no. 635 (1907): 331.

3. Louis Alloro, "A Magical Day of Inquiry, Scholarship, and Practice," *Positive Psychology News,* April 25, 2012, positivepsychologynews.com/news/louis-alloro/2012042521852.

4. Matthew Rees, "How to Win Like Michael Phelps," *Wall Street Journal,* June 22, 2016, wsj.com/articles/how-to-win-like-michael-phelps-1466635351.

5. "UNDER ARMOUR | RULE YOURSELF | MICHAEL PHELPS," YouTube video, 1:31, posted by "Under Armour," March 8, 2016, youtube.com/watch?v=Xh9jAD1ofm4.

6. Shirley S. Wang, "To Stop Procrastinating, Start by Understanding the Emotions Involved," *Wall Street Journal,* August 31, 2015, wsj.com/articles/to-stop-procrastinating-start-by-understanding-whats-really-going-on-1441043167.

7. Peter M. Gollwitzer, "Implementation Intentions: Strong Effects of Simple Plans," *American Psychologist* 54, no. 7 (July 1999): 493–503.

8. Shirley S. Wang, "To Stop Procrastinating, Start by Understanding the Emotions Involved."

9. William J. Knaus, *Do It Now! Break the Procrastination Habit,* (Hoboken, NJ: John Wiley & Sons, 2001).

10. Druss, "The Victor Hugo working naked story: myth or fact?," Languor.us (blog), August 20, 2012, languor.us/victor-hugo-working-naked-story-myth-or-fact.

11. Shirley S. Wang, "To Stop Procrastinating, Start by Understanding the Emotions Involved."

12. Maria Parker (U.S. long-distance cyclist), interview with Caroline Adams Miller, February 17, 2016.

13. Robert M. Sapolsky, "Language Shapes Thoughts—and Storm Preparations," *Wall Street Journal,* April 22, 2015.

14. Susan Pinker, "For Better Performance, Give Yourself a Pep Talk," *Wall Street Journal,* July 27, 2016, wsj.com/articles/for-better-performance-give-yourself-a-pep-talk-1469633065; Gretchen Reynolds, "Keep Telling Yourself, 'This Workout Feels Good,'" *New York Times,* November 6, 2013, well.blogs.nytimes.com/2013/11/06/keep-repeating-this-workout-feels-good/.

15. Chris Ballard, "Ryan Anderson tries to move forward after girlfriend Gia Allemand's suicide," *Sports Illustrated,* November 17, 2014.

16. Jack Nicklaus made this remark during the 2016 US Open while the rain delays made the course almost unplayable, saying that if a player complained about the weather, Nicklaus's experience had shown him that they were mentally out of the game at that point and would probably no longer be a factor.

17. Kevin Clark, "The NFL's Best Method Actor," *Wall Street Journal,* December 1, 2015, wsj.com/articles/meet-the-nfls-best-method-actor-1449002579.

18. Caitlin McCabe, "Virtual Reality Therapy Shows New Benefits," *Wall Street Journal,* October 20, 2014, wsj.com/articles/virtual-reality-therapy-shows-new-benefits-1413841124.

19. R. L. Reid, "The psychology of the near miss," *Journal of Gambling Behavior* 2, no. 1 (March 1986): 32–39.

20. J.K. Rowling, "Text of J.K. Rowling's Speech: 'The Fringe Benefits of Failure, and the Importance of Imagination,'" *Harvard Gazette,* June 5, 2008, news.harvard.edu/gazette/story/2008/06/text-of-j-k-rowling-speech/.

21. Tony Schwartz, "The Rhythm of Great Performance," *New York Times,* February 27, 2015, nytimes.com/2015/02/28/business/dealbook/the-rhythm-of-great-performance.html.

22. Katheen Elkins, "Here's why Tim Cook, Sallie Krawcheck and other successful people wake up at 4 a.m.," CNBC.com, August 29, 2016, cnbc.com/2016/08/29/why-tim-cook-sallie-krawcheck-and-other-successful-people-wake-up-at-4-am.html; Kathleen Elkins, "A man who spent 5 years studying millionaires found one of their most important wealth-building habits starts first thing in the morning," *Business Insider,* April 7, 2016, businessinsider.com/rich-people-wake-up-early-2016-4.

23. Tony Schwartz, "The Rhythm of Great Performance."

24. Karlyn Pipes (author and International Hall of Fame swimmer), interview with Caroline Adams Miller, February 14, 2015.

25. Roy Baumeister (professor at Florida State University), interview with Caroline Adams Miller, February 12, 2007.

26. "The Zeigarnick Effect: Drive to Finish and Need for Closure—Business, Marketing . . . Spielberg, Lucas, Rowling . . .," BizShifts-Trends.com (blog), August 16, 2012, bizshifts-trends.com/tag/zeigarnik-effect/.

27. "SC Featured: The Volunteer," ESPN.com video, 6:57, posted February 29, 2016, espn.com/video/clip?id=14859845.

28. Robert Lee Holtz, "Practice Personalities: What an Avatar Can Teach You," *Wall Street Journal,* January 19, 2015, wsj.com/articles/ practice-personalities-what-an-avatar-can-teach-you-1421703480.

Chapter 15   Patience

1. Dennis Overbye, "Gravitational Waves Detected, Confirming Einstein's Theory," *New York Times,* February 11, 2016, nytimes.com/2016/02/12/ science/ligo-gravitational-waves-black-holes-einstein.html?_r=0.

2. Khushbu Shah, "How to Order Domino's Pizza With a Pizza Emoji," *Eater.com,* May 13, 2015, eater.com/2015/5/13/8597819/ how-to-order-dominos-pizza-emoji.

3. Christopher Muther, "Instant gratification is making us perpetually impatient," *Boston Globe,* February 2, 2013.

4. Ibid.

5. Ibid.

6. Stephanie Rosenbloom, "The World According to Tim Ferriss," *New York Times,* March 25, 2011, nytimes.com/2011/03/27/fashion/27Ferris.html.

7. Pamela Druckerman, "Why French Parents Are Superior," *Wall Street Journal,* February 4, 2012, wsj.com/articles/SB100014240529702047409 04577196931457473816.

8. Leonard Sax, "For readers of the *Wall Street Journal,*" LeonardSax.com, leonardsax.com/WSJ.htm.

9. Julie Scelfo, "Suicide on Campus and the Pressure of Perfection," *New York Times,* July 27, 2015, nytimes.com/2015/08/02/education/edlife/ stress-social-media-and-suicide-on-campus.html.

10. Anonymous middle school psychologist, interview with Caroline Adams Miller, February 5, 2016.

11. Matthew Schneier, "The Post-Binge-Watching-Blues: A Malady of Our Times," *New York Times,* December 5, 2015, nytimes.com/2015/12/06/ fashion/post-binge-watching-blues.html.

12. Christopher Clarey, "Every Second Counts in Bid to Keep Sports Fans," *New York Times,* February 28, 2015.

13. Ibid.

14. William C. Rhoden, "For Coaches, It's Nurture vs. Natural Talent," *New York Times,* April 6, 2015, nytimes.com/2015/04/07/sports/ncaabasketball/for-coaches-its-nurture-vs-natural-talent.html.

15. Christina Rexrode, "Citigroup to Millennial Bankers: Take a Year Off," *Wall Street Journal,* March 16, 2016, wsj.com/articles/to-entice-millennial-bankers-citigroup-serves-up-new-perk-take-a-year-off-1458120603.

16. Rachel Feintzeig, "Lavish Perks Spawn New Job Category," *Wall Street Journal,* November 20, 2014, wsj.com/articles/lavish-perks-spawn-new-job-category-1416529198.

17. Nick McGreivy (University of Pennsylvania student), interview with Caroline Adams Miller, February 17, 2016.

18. Ginger Rae Dunbar, "Youth learn to focus, have patience from playing chess," *Reporter,* December 9, 2014, thereporteronline.com/article/RO/20141209/NEWS/141209802.

19. Cal Newport, "Cal Newport on Deep Work," interview by Scotty Barry Kaufman, *Psychology Podcast,* podcast audio, June 11, 2016, thepsychologypodcast.com/?s=Newport.

20. Dan Buettner, "Want Great Longevity and Health? It Takes a Village," *Wall Street Journal,* May 22, 2015, wsj.com/articles/want-great-longevity-and-health-it-takes-a-village-1432304395.

21. Chelsea Harvey, "Why living around nature could make you live longer," *Washington Post,* April 19, 2016.

22. Tyler Cowen, "The Upside of Waiting in Line," *New York Times,* February 19, 2015, nytimes.com/2015/02/22/upshot/the-upside-of-waiting-in-line.html.

23. Xianchi Dai and Ayelet Fishbach, "When waiting to choose increases patience," *Organizational Behavior and Human Decision Processes* 121, no. 2 (July 2013): 256–266.

24. Jennifer L. Roberts, "The Power of Patience," *Harvard Magazine,* November–December 2013, harvardmagazine.com/2013/11/the-power-of-patience.

About the Author

for almost three decades, Caroline Adams Miller, MAPP, has been a pioneer with her groundbreaking work in the areas of addiction, well-being, and success. She is one of the first people to get a master's degree in the science of applied positive psychology and is recognized as one of the world's leading experts on the science linking happiness, goal-setting, and grit. Caroline speaks to audiences around the world and maintains a thriving executive coaching practice focused on goal accomplishment. She has taught in a number of schools and is a guest lecturer at the Wharton School Executive MBA program. She is also one of the first happiness experts to join and advise Happify, the world's largest pioneering online tool dedicated to assessing and amplifying well-being through evidence-based games and activities. Caroline is the author of five books, including *Positively Caroline, My Name Is Caroline,* and *Creating Your Best Life,* and has been featured in hundreds of magazines, newspapers, and other media outlets worldwide, including the *New York Times,* the *Washington Post, USA Today, US News & World Report,* ABC, CBS, NBC, NPR, and CNN. She was the first positive psychology expert on satellite radio with her "Positive Tip of the Day" and in 2013 won the Mentoring award from the George Washington University School of Business for her decades of helping others achieve their goals. Caroline graduated magna cum laude from Harvard University and is a black belt in Hapkido and a top-ranked Masters swimmer in multiple events. She resides with her husband, Haywood, outside Washington, DC, and has three grown children and an adorable schnoodle named Alpha.

About Sounds True

Sounds True is a multimedia publisher whose mission is to inspire and support personal transformation and spiritual awakening. Founded in 1985 and located in Boulder, Colorado, we work with many of the leading spiritual teachers, thinkers, healers, and visionary artists of our time. We strive with every title to preserve the essential "living wisdom" of the author or artist. It is our goal to create products that not only provide information to a reader or listener, but that also embody the quality of a wisdom transmission.

For those seeking genuine transformation, Sounds True is your trusted partner. At SoundsTrue.com you will find a wealth of free resources to support your journey, including exclusive weekly audio interviews, free downloads, interactive learning tools, and other special savings on all our titles.

To learn more, please visit SoundsTrue.com/freegifts or call us toll-free at 800.333.9185.